EARTH ALCHEMY

First published and distributed in the United Kingdom by:
Hay House UK Ltd, Astley House, 33 Notting Hill Gate, London W11 3JQ
Tel: +44 (0)20 3675 2450; Fax: +44 (0)20 3675 2451
www.hayhouse.co.uk

Published and distributed in the United States of America by:
Hay House Inc., PO Box 5100, Carlsbad, CA 92018-5100
Tel: (1) 760 431 7695 or (800) 654 5126
Fax: (1) 760 431 6948 or (800) 650 5115
www.hayhouse.com

Published and distributed in Australia by:
Hay House Australia Ltd, 18/36 Ralph St, Alexandria NSW 2015
Tel: (61) 2 9669 4299; Fax: (61) 2 9669 4144
www.hayhouse.com.au

Published and distributed in the Republic of South Africa by:
Hay House SA (Pty) Ltd, PO Box 990, Witkoppen 2068
Tel/Fax: (27) 11 467 8904
www.hayhouse.co.za

Published and distributed in India by:
Hay House Publishers India, Muskaan Complex, Plot No.3, B-2,
Vasant Kunj, New Delhi 110 070
Tel: (91) 11 4176 1620; Fax: (91) 11 4176 1630
www.hayhouse.co.in

Distributed in Canada by:
Raincoast, 9050 Shaughnessy St, Vancouver BC V6P 6E5 Tel: (1) 604 323 7100;
Fax: (1) 604 323 2600

A catalogue record for this book is available from the British Library.

ISBN 978-1-78180-234-2

EARTH ALCHEMY

A Dynamic Fusion Between Alchemy and the Eight Celtic Festivals

GLENNIE KINDRED

HAY HOUSE

Carlsbad, California • New York City • London • Sydney
Johannesburg • Vancouver • Hong Kong • New Delhi

CONTENTS

Dedicated to Howard Salt

29 April 1956–25 May 2005

In celebration of his courage to transform his past.

I am at One with my path again and it is good
As laughing

With Love and Gratitude

With Love and gratitude to the Earth, my teacher, guide and anchor.

With Love and gratitude to the Spirit of Hermes Mercurius, a constant source of inspiration and synergy, reminding me that there is more to Life than meets the eye.

With Love and gratitude to Michelle Pilley at Hay House UK for giving me the opportunity to write this book. It has been a great pleasure and delight to work with you. Also my thanks and appreciation to all the team at Hay House UK, especially to Duncan Carson for all your help in bringing the new edition of this book into being.

With Love and gratitude to my family, whose Love and generosity of Spirit are always there for me: to my wonderful mum, Margaret Newman, for inspiring me to jump into Life and live it to the full; to my dearest friend and partner, Brian Boothby, for sharing the journey with me; and to my children, Jerry Pollett and Jack and May Kindred Boothby, and granddaughter Evie Rose Pollett, for sharing your lives with me.

With Love and gratitude to all my sacred kin and close friends, especially to the Elementals for the deep sharing, honesty, support and Love of true friendship and true alchemy.

I send this Love and gratitude out into the Web of Life, where it continues to grow.

Walking as Before

We have always been walking through this land.
We have always worn its vision like a skin,
but on the inside.
There has never been a time
when this river has not chilled our veins.
The track is strongly felt.
We are walking, we are walking as before
and our footsteps fit.
We pass that fragile moment
when everything becomes
itself but more so.
Look to each other across chasms of ancient time.
We are moving round a single unchanging point.
Move to the very edge
where the old world ends
and something else begins ...

And we have always been walking through this land
And we have always worn its vision like a skin
The track is strongly felt, walking as before
And our footsteps fit, walking as before
Move to the very edge where the old world ends
And something else begins, something else begins
Move to the very edge where the old world ends
And something else begins, something else begins ...

By Carolyn Hillyer

Preface

Most of us have heard of the popular myth of alchemists attempting to turn base metal into Gold, and their search for the Philosopher's Stone and the Elixir of Life. For years I looked into books on alchemy and could make no sense of it. It seemed to be cloaked in intellectualism, complex concepts and puzzling symbolism, but I continued to be intrigued because of a personal connection I made many years ago to Hermes Mercurius, the Greek and Roman messenger of the gods and a key figure in alchemy. Through my deepening understanding of Hermes Mercurius, my passion for metaphysics, and my passion for following the cycle of the year through the eight Celtic festivals, I found a key that opened the door to alchemy. I began to see that the alchemist's journey through each of the alchemical experiences was similar to my journey through the Wheel of the Year with the eight Celtic festivals. I then had a 'eureka' moment, when I realised that each of the main alchemical processes were the same intrinsic energy pattern as each of the eight Celtic festivals, and so I was able to understand them perfectly from this perspective. My journey through the Wheel of the Year has been greatly deepened by this fusion of the two systems and this book grew from that union.

There are no fixed doctrines in alchemy. It is based on simple observations of natural laws that root it firmly in the Earth, in the self and in the journey itself. This too is the same as following the Celtic festivals. We may call them 'Celtic' festivals or 'pagan' festivals, for they began in the past, but they continue today, uniquely evolving and developing to reflect the changing times. We each celebrate and honour them in our own way. There is no hierarchy, no one telling us how to celebrate them. We do what feels right and good for ourselves and this deepens our personal philosophy and spirituality and our relationship with the Earth. Similarly every alchemist takes their own unique path, beginning with what they know and developing through what they discover. As part of an ongoing process, each alchemist integrates their experiences with their own personal spiritual development, growth and understanding, earthing this in their own personal philosophy – their Philosopher's Stone.

Every alchemist brings their own personal interests to their experience of alchemy. My background is in working with the energy of the Earth's cycles through the eight Celtic festivals, and the Five Elements, and a great love of metaphysics and so this is what I bring to it. I also bring my natural passion for the transformative power of Universal or Unconditional Love as a force for healing and change in our lives and in the world.

Celebrating each of the Celtic festivals (see chart on page 27) brings stability and inner reflection into my life so that I am in touch with my spiritual development and my connection to the Earth through the unfolding cycle of the year. Similarly the alchemist's journey is rooted in the same natural cycles of union, birth, death and rebirth. The journey is always circular. There are always endings, whether created by choice, by Time, by circumstances, or by the seasonal cycle, but each ending opens up a new beginning and each time the journey deepens, as new cycles of understanding grow from within.

Through celebrating the Earth's cycles I am rooted in my environment and myself. I unite with the seasonal energy of the Earth and so experience myself as part of the Unity of life. Through this I am connected to each of the Five Elements of life: Earth, Air, Fire, Water and Quintessence or Spirit, which is the unifying element that is in all life. This is the Infinite and Eternal Force, the Essence and the Source of life and it is this that the alchemist ultimately seeks to experience – the Gold! As well as being rooted in the physical world, the Five Elements are an essential energy language and I experience them as mutable connectors of energy, an interface between Matter and Spirit. This interface is where alchemy happens, where energy merges and re-forms, transforms and transmutes. The quest for the alchemist's Gold is to experience our wholeness and our Oneness and Unity with all of Life.

This consciousness of the Unity of life has been part of my life's quest and has been growing ever stronger during the last 30 years. I see it as the path to our planetary healing, as well as to our own wellbeing and lasting happiness. As an alchemist,

I aim to unite all parts of myself, to embrace the invisible as well as the visible, the acceptable as well as the unexplained. I follow my feelings and my intuition; I follow my imagination into the world within me. I look at what is hidden, reading between the lines, searching for the common bonds and the roots of communion, the paths that create Unity and Harmony. I seek my true connection to Universal Love and Inner Peace as the root of my happiness and health – the Elixir of Life!

I see my life as a gift, to be grasped with both hands. I feel like an adventurer or great explorer, even though much of my life has been home-based, bringing up children. I feel like a pioneer, even though I am probably covering the same ground as many others before me. It doesn't matter. I am on my own journey, living my own life, which is unfolding from my own choices.

This book is an account of a year (2004) and the alchemy I experienced within the Earth's yearly cycle, fusing the alchemical experiences with the Celtic festivals. To write this book, I had to start somewhere, but of course my journey began many years ago and this is just a window into what is part of many yearly cycles that have gone before and part of many cycles that will follow... for all things are connected.

I give thanks for the journey.

Glennie Kindred, 2013

The Gift of Strong Roots
An Introduction to Alchemy

Alchemy is rooted in the Earth and the natural Regenerative Force that constantly creates and manifests Life. Alchemy is the force of transformation that is Life itself.

To become an alchemist is to actively engage with transformation, to work with the Fertile Life Force of Nature that we are all part of; to actively create new Life from Union and co-operation with this creative force.

Alchemy is firmly rooted in the interconnected Web of Life. The alchemist celebrates the richness of Life's diversity and each individual. It is a path of inclusion and wholeness, and ultimately an experience of the Gold, the Unity of Oneness with all things.

The History of Alchemy

Alchemy has a long and varied history that spans many ages, cultures and civilizations. The strength of alchemy lies in these deep roots that go far back in Time. Alchemy is a study of the art of transformation and, true to itself, it has transformed many times, surviving the changing political and religious climates of many centuries. Its early roots are in the ancient civilizations of China and Egypt and by the fifth century AD it was known as 'the Divine Art' or 'the Sacred Art' in China, India, South East Asia, Japan and the Far East. The early alchemists were philosophers and healers searching for the Elixir of Life. They understood that mind, body and Spirit were One and that personal philosophy was as much a part of healing and longevity as the elixirs they were creating. The search for Gold may have begun as a metaphor for the most precious thing we have, our health.

The early Chinese alchemists were Taoists who aimed to keep the energy flowing through the body and saw this as a key to prolonging life. They worked with three vital energies: Chi, the Life Force; Ching, the Vital Essence; and Sheen, breath control.

Indian alchemy was influenced by Hinduism and, like its Chinese counterpart, sought to prolong life, in this case through Yoga and Tantra, seeking to cleanse the body and mind through breath control (Prana) and work with the seven chakras. They aimed to release energies latent in the body to gain enlightenment and absolute freedom from the confines of Time.

Alchemy came to Europe in the Middle Ages, probably after the First Crusade (1095–1099). The search for the Holy Grail and the Chalice grew from this period of cultural fusion. Early alchemical texts were translated from the Arabic into Latin. The most famous of these is The Emerald Tablet, which originated in Egypt (see Appendix, page 273). This important yet simple text is still used by alchemists today and is thought by many to hold the keys to alchemy.

We all have an image of the archaic alchemist in his laboratory, heating flasks and trying to turn base metal into Gold. This is only part of the picture and needs to be understood in context. Gold was valued as a great gift from the Earth Mother. Its beauty, its malleability and its non-corrosive properties made it a valuable metal of exchange. It was also valued for its purity and its healing properties and it was known as the Master Healer. In the past all smiths, especially goldsmiths, were considered to be shamans, spiritual teachers, great magicians, poets and healers, and alchemists inherit all of these aspects of themselves in their quest for Gold. (See Appendix, page 263)

In early times it was believed that all metals were 'growing' and would eventually become Gold. The early alchemists believed they could speed up this natural process and devised many experiments to do this. I am struck by their belief that it was possible, as this points to a basic belief in our ability to transmute Matter, the essence of alchemical thought and healing.

The medieval alchemists of Europe, many of them women, worked with a system based on seven chemical processes or operations, which were linked to seven metals and seven planets. In this way the metals and minerals found in the Earth were united with the heavens as part of the 'Great Work' of alchemy. At this time the planets were understood to be Gods and Goddesses, each infused with a unique energy. To understand these different energies they were given personalities and from this we inherit a wealth of legends, myths and symbolism. The early alchemists would have also been astrologers and believed, as astrologers still do today, that life on Earth is influenced by each of the planets as they move through the heavens.

In alchemy great importance has always been placed on the equality of women and men. Many female alchemists would work with a mystic brother and male alchemists would work with a mystic sister. This was also extended to include the balance of the male and female within each person and the balance of the active self and the receptive self.

To understand medieval alchemy, we need to appreciate the political, religious and scientific climate of the times. Medieval alchemy was a fusion of the earlier alchemical texts, the philosophical minds of the day, the growth of Christianity and the rising power of the medieval Church. It was also influenced by the climate of new scientific discoveries such as the distillation process, which led to healing elixirs being made from plant and mineral extracts. With its introduction into Europe, alchemy seems to have begun to lose touch with its metaphysical and spiritual roots and to have become more concerned with chemistry.

Out of this climate of science and experimentation came alchemists who were obsessed with the creation of Gold from base metals such as Lead, Mercury or Silver. These pseudo-alchemists, or false alchemists, were referred to as 'Puffers', relating to their puffed-up egos and their obsession with puffing up the fires in their laboratories in an attempt to transmute other substances into Gold. They are a lasting example of where alchemists can go wrong. In many ways, though, this helped the true alchemists, who were able to quietly continue with their personal quest for inner Gold.

From the Middle Ages onwards alchemy became cloaked in intrigue, secrets and hidden codes. The alchemical processes, which had begun as an exploration of natural laws and chemical reactions, were now hidden in metaphor and symbolism. This was an attempt to disguise what the powerful medieval Church condemned as heretical, since alchemy was based on the belief that individuals could develop their own spiritual path without the intervention and control of the Church. Alchemy was also condemned for its radical inclusion of sexuality as a natural route to experiencing the Divine.

Alchemical ideas surfaced again in the Renaissance through the art, poetry and philosophical writings of the time.

Many alchemists were also Christians and they developed their alchemical philosophy alongside their Christianity. The philosophers and intellectuals of the day combined science, natural magic, mathematics, astrology and medicine with their belief in the Astral Planes and Angelic Realms. Humanity was seen as part of the Unity of Nature, integrated within a greater cosmology and higher intelligence.

However, again alchemy was forced underground by the powerful authority of the Church, which encouraged a very different view of spirituality. Its polarized view of Heaven and Hell and good and evil was in direct opposition to alchemy's essential belief in Unity. Gradually the mystical, esoteric and metaphysical side of alchemy retreated behind closed doors. Over the centuries its interest in metals and chemistry waned and the alchemical processes developed as philosophical and psychological experiences.

Alchemy surfaced again as part of the nineteenth-century spiritual revival. Once again it was seen as an inner journey of the Soul and the emphasis was now firmly on our selves as the vessel for the 'Great Work'. Through the work of the Golden Dawn and the College of Psychic Studies, which began in London in 1887, the mystical and the magical aspects of alchemy and the use of the imagination as a path to the Gold were explored and belief in the essential Unity of Life was revived.

In the 1920s the work of Carl Jung took alchemy to another level. Jung recognized the symbols and images of the old alchemical texts as being the symbolic language of dreams and archetypes common to us all. He viewed this as coming from the 'collective unconscious' and concluded that alchemy was about the development of the psyche of the alchemist. Jung himself worked with what he called the process of 'individuation', the journey of an individual's Soul towards wholeness from the roots of the psyche.

Alchemy has been continuing to develop these psychological and mystical threads throughout the twentieth century and into the twenty-first century. The work has evolved and grown over the years. There are now many more alchemical processes than the original seven and because it is the work of each individual, every alchemist has a different order and unique interpretation. There are also many alchemists with no interest in working with the old alchemical processes or the old alchemical texts, those who have developed their own systems, and those who are natural alchemists and healers. The growth of metaphysics and holistic medicine has opened the door to a new understanding of alchemy and a new generation of alchemists.

Alchemy continues to develop and evolve and is always inclusive of what each Age and each alchemist brings to it. This is what makes alchemy so exciting. It is a living dynamic journey that is evolving with us.

The Alchemy of Symbols

Throughout its history alchemy has developed a wealth of symbols, symbolic metaphor and its own symbolic language. This encourages the brain to function alchemically through the imagination, the intuition and creativity. Much of the symbolism found in historical texts was meant to obscure the spiritual significance of alchemy at a time when the Church was a political authority and condemned any other route to the Divine. Writing in the twenty-first century, there is no need for me to cloak my words in codes and intrigue. I am seeking clarity of meaning and therefore my use of symbols is more about their energetic use.

Symbols work alchemically, creating Unity and transformation by linking the conscious with the unconscious and back again in continuous circuits that cut through into new levels of understanding. They help us to move from our left brain, our logical, rational 'outer' way of thinking, to our right brain, our intuitive, receptive, 'inner' way of understanding. A symbol acts as a bridge and a connecting link and it helps us to transcend to new levels of understanding. Its meaning is not fixed by words, and our understanding is free to develop, change and grow.

A symbol can hold much information, ideas and concepts simultaneously, with many layers of meaning and information. It can be used as a memory aid. Whole bodies of information and concepts can be passed on in a simple symbol. This is seen in each of the astrological symbols, the symbols for each planet and those of the Runes or Ogham. These are all currencies of communication that unite people through their common knowledge. Many symbols we still use today are very ancient and hold layers of meaning and influences from other times and other cultures.

Symbols are easily retained by the mind because they engage both sides of the brain. They have Life, movement and energy. Their vibration is almost tangible, on the edge between Matter and Spirit. They fire up our active imagination; they open doorways to new insights and new levels of understanding and to transformation that we may have difficulty expressing in words.

A symbol can be sent and received in an instant. Some healing systems use symbols to create an energy web or energy share that open up channels of healing energy. Symbols are also used to draw in energy or create a connection. They can be used as a focus for meditation and contemplation. Keeping the mind centred on a symbol helps to unlock the energy held within it and to still the mind so that it is able to transcend itself.

Sometimes I 'receive' a symbol in a meditation or from an inner journey. It creates a link to my subconscious or to an inner Spirit Guide. I have been working with some symbols for years and there are always new insights to be gained as their layers of meaning surface from deep within me. I can understand a symbol on one level and then break through to a new level of understanding which includes and also transcends the earlier meaning. This is what makes symbols so exciting to work with.

The following are alchemical symbols which are still in use today.

The Yin Yang

This is a universally recognized symbol of harmony, balance and Unity that is at the heart of alchemy because it reflects balance and flowing energy.

The dark side is Yin, associated with receptivity, intuition, the Moon, Water, fluidity, mutability, the unconscious, the inner world and roots.

The light side is Yang, associated with action, expansion, the Sun, Fire, the conscious, rational and logical thinking, the outer world, expressed energy, manifestation and visible growth.

Each part has a doorway into its opposite side through the opposite-coloured dot. This is balance in motion, unrestricted, unlimited and unbound. The Yin Yang symbol is a model of the fluidity and freedom of movement that is necessary for harmony, Unity and balance to exist. Balance needs fluidity and freedom so that its natural route to equilibrium is open.

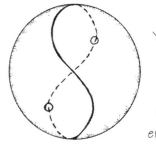

The energy path of the Yin Yang symbol can also be drawn as an Infinity symbol, when the two dots are seen as part of a three-dimensional circuit linking the energy of Yin and Yang to each other, creating equilibrium in motion. Harmony is freedom!

Luna and Sol

The old alchemical texts are full of the interrelated dance of Luna and Sol, the symbolic Union and equality of the Moon and the Sun.

The Sun represents Yang, our conscious mind, our logical and rational thought processes and left-brain activity.

In the symbolism of alchemy Sol is the King and is linked to the element of Fire, the initiator of transformation. His colour and metal are Gold and he invites us to act, to aim for the highest, the purest, the most worthy. Other symbols linked to Sol are the Lion, the Fire Dragon, Salamander and Phoenix. Sol represents our ego, our power of free will and choice, and our actions in the world.

The Moon represents Yin, our unconscious mind, the right-brain activity that takes us beyond logic to experience our feelings, our sixth sense, inner listening, intuition, telepathy, receptivity, the path of the heart and Universal Love.

In the symbolism of alchemy Luna is the Queen who rules the dark deep unconscious parts of our lives and her colour and metal are Silver. She is linked to the element Water and is the essence of receptivity and reflection, holding the doorway open to communication beyond the surface of reality. She is the Silver Lady, Lady Alchymia and Luna Woman who asks me to feel and not to speak, to seek within for the answers to Life's mysteries, to internalize my experiences, to interpret and absorb the wisdom held within them. The alchemy of Luna consciousness helps me to open up the intuitive way, explore what this natural part of myself has to tell me, to bring this intelligence into a place of balance in my life.

The Union between Luna and Sol is the symbolic 'Chymical Wedding' of alchemy, the balance and Union between the female and the male, the unconscious and the conscious, Yin and Yang. The Chymical Wedding is also a personal act of alchemy as we unite our outer self with our inner self. This union creates an experience of the interface or opening we find within ourselves when we unite our conscious actions with our receptivity and intuition. This is our seventh sense, our Spirit path.

The Vesica Piscis

The Vesica Piscis is a symbolic model of alchemy and the art of transformation through Union. The place where the two overlapping circles of energy come together, overlap, the opening, the petal or doorway at the centre, is the interface where the two separate parts merge into One. This upright oval opening at the centre of the Vesica Piscis is known as the Mandorla or Vesica and represents a threshold, a point of transition. It is often used in mystical art to surround a sacred figure with Light and symbolizes transmutation into Spirit or Unity with Spirit. This is the place of creation, where a dynamic new energy grows from the Union of the two. It is a place of transition, where energy changes and becomes something new. I consciously explore this in-between place, where energy is fluid, blending and integrating, this place of transition, Unity and alchemy.

The Caduceus

In alchemy the Caduceus, the healing symbol of Unity, is carried by Hermes Mercurius. It is an ancient symbol of healing that is still used today and is most often known as a symbol for homoeopathy and healing practices that bring together the Unity of mind, body and Spirit, the holistic approach to healing.

The entwined black and white snakes or serpents rise up the central stem, the Staff of Unity or Wand of Power that represents the usable energy and power of the Life Force. The Caduceus represents our ability to heal any separation through Unity. Once we find Unity in ourselves we are able to take this healing out into the world and bring it to others.

The Caduceus has wings to signify transcendence, awakened spiritual energy, movement, rising above the material world into Spirit. We are all transcendent beings; we all have wings to fly to the Spirit Realms, the realms of our imagination and the realms of our thoughts. We can all use our thoughts consciously to direct and influence our lives and to open up the channels to healing ourselves and others. When I remember that I am transcendental, I become this Unity and this fluidity as part of my whole self and my own healing.

As Above, So Below
As Within, So Without

This is probably the most famous of the alchemical maxims and reminds us of the essential Unity between our inner world and our outer world. Whatever we do in the physical world simultaneously resonates and influences the inner world and whatever is on the inside, in our hearts and minds, is reflected into the outer world.

We are not separate, but united, communicating, flowing and merging on many different levels of Life. Our actions are not isolated and we do not live only in linear Time, but cyclic Time, with never-ending cycles of endings and new beginnings, a matrix of overlapping cycles that create openings and doorways where integrated moments meet. I look for where they touch in my life, where they manifest as synchronicity, coincidence and telepathy. These are the doorways I jump through and experience as places of interface, integration and alchemy.

Everything we do, say and think is an opportunity to live our lives from this place of balance and integration, uniting our spiritual path with our everyday lives.

The Philosopher's Stone

The alchemist's goal or Gold lies in experiencing the Unity of Life, in feeling part of the interconnected Web of energy that is the Essence of Life. Essentially, we are all alchemists and we all possess the Gold, the Elixir of Life and the Philosopher's Stone – as soon as we recognize it. It may only be fleeting glimpse, but each time we find our connection to this Gold, this Unity within us, we know how it feels and we can find it again.

All alchemists work as individuals within the Unity of all Life and alchemy is about honouring our own originality and responsibility to ourselves as well as our responsibility to the whole, the Web of Life around us. In this way it leads us to explore where we are separated from this wholeness and to heal our past and therefore our present and our future. For they are One whole, the same Unity.

Alchemy is about trusting ourselves and our own basic goodness. It is non-judgemental, accepting that we grow, change and learn through our experiences. It is not about completion, but about the journey. We bring to it our own perspectives, emotions and who we are at this point in Time. It is a journey of self-discovery that asks of us the courage to be truly honest with ourselves. This leads naturally to change and transformation. The alchemy happens inside us first and spreads outwards from there.

Alchemy encourages the use of intuition, meditation and the imagination to balance our reliance on logical thinking.

It encourages the deep parts of ourselves to come to the surface so that we truly experience our whole selves.

Alchemy is energy in motion. Emotional and mental stagnation, particularly when we harbour old hurts and negative feelings, create much damage both within ourselves and through the negative energy that is then sent out into the world. Alchemy restores balance and harmony within us and this is then reflected out into the continuous cycles of changing energy and transformation that we create.

Alchemy investigates the creative energy released through Union, especially the Union of opposite forces or opposite parts of ourselves. Out of Union comes new energy and movement, new Life, new beginnings. It is this place, this interface where new beginnings are forming, that interests the alchemist and healer, for it is here that we can join the dance and participate in the energy and Spirit of transformation.

The Alchemy of Love and Healing

Alchemy is the conscious use of energy. I believe that everything that exists is an interconnected stream of energy and we do nothing in isolation. We are connected to all of Life always and the energy of Life is always cyclic. What we send, we receive.

As an alchemist I become the Unity that I seek. I consciously send out Unity and therefore draw it towards myself, opening up the connection to the Web or Matrix, the Essence and the Source of Life. I use the word 'Matrix' to create a link to understanding Life as a circuit of interconnected energy from which all Matter takes form, and in its ancient context, from the Latin mater, meaning 'mother' and 'womb', the Creatress, Mother of Life.

As an alchemist I also consciously create loving energy, which is the source of my happiness and well-being and strengthens my Life Force or Chi. By sending out Love I contribute to the increase of Love circulating in the world. I am convinced that whatever we put our attention towards increases. In this way Love creates more Love and harmony creates more harmony. This also links us to all the Love and happiness that we have ever experienced. We sustain the energy by becoming One with the Universal Love available to all. One act of Love links us to the whole. We pass Love on in cycles of goodwill and kindness and bring increase with every positive and loving action we make. By the same token the reverse is true... We are all therefore responsible for the world we create, not just in our personal lives but as contributors to the energy that is at large in the world.

We are also all receptive to the alchemy of healing and transformation. Healing energy can be felt, it can be sent to ourselves and to others. We can create vibrational energy that has great transformative healing power by our use of Unconditional Love, by the vibration we set in motion through our words, thoughts and emotions. We aid the alchemy of

healing by our positive attitude and we can enhance our Life Force through energy work, through the Life Force present in the food we eat and through conscious breath work.

I become aware of my energy field by closing my eyes and sending my energy out as far as it will go. I experience myself as formless and limitless energy, unconfined by Time and Matter. I can send myself across to the other side of the world or out into space. I can leave this world and enter the internal world of my imagination to become One with Spirit in all things, to transmute illness, to meet Guardian Angels, Spirit Guides or Nature Spirits. If I imagine it, then I experience it and it has Life.

The Alchemy of the Chakra System

This is a system that stems from the Hindu and Buddhist metaphysical tradition and has become part of my alchemical journey at this time.

Traditionally, the seven chakras are energy centres of the subtle or ethereal body, the Spirit body that co-exists with the physical body. They can be imagined as a series of doorways or portals that give access to the body's internal energy system. The energy of each chakra cannot be seen in the normal way but with practice can be felt and 'seen' with the inner eye.

Illness manifests first as imbalance in our subtle bodies

and in our chakras and will eventually manifest in the greater density of our physical bodies. Learning to work at the subtle energy level greatly adds to our potential for self-healing. There is a chart and brief summary of the chakras and how to work with them in the Appendix (page 259).

The Earth and Her Cycles

I have been working alchemically within the framework of the Earth's cycles for a long time now. Alchemy has been part of my life, without the label, for many years. I came to it long after my journey with the Earth's cycles began, but was instantly able to understand the alchemical processes on an energetic level through my understanding of the Celtic festivals.

I have called the alchemical processes 'experiences' and they directly link in energy to each of the eight Celtic festivals. Union, the most important of the experiences, occurs naturally twice in the Earth's cycle, at each of the Equinoxes.

This book is an exploration of this fusion of alchemy and the eight Celtic festivals. This gives me two complementary systems that both have an underlying belief in the interconnected Unity of Life. Both also explore the energy of Spirit in Matter and both work with the natural cyclic energy of Life. The fusion of the two puts the alchemical cycle into the cycle of the year and the seasons, so that my understanding and experience of alchemy are linked to the underlying energy of the Earth.

For me, each of the Celtic festivals lasts for several weeks and over a period of time I do a variety of things that help me to connect to the Earth's energy and my own journey. Each festival comes as a reminder to take some time out for myself, to remember my spiritual path and how this is unfolding in my life. This helps me to become aware of what I am feeling at a very deep level. Alchemy and the Celtic festivals are both self-empowering and self-motivating, and each complements the other.

HERMES MERCURIUS

Hermes Mercurius is a key figure found throughout alchemical texts, an archetypal energy that reoccurs in many different cultures. I have used a blending name that links two of them: 'Hermes' from the Greek and 'Mercury' or 'Mercurius' from the Roman. The same energy found in ancient Egypt is called Thoth and in the Norse tradition it is known as Odin or Woden.

Clues to the essence of this energy are found in the chemical substance Mercury or Quicksilver, which is a heavy metallic liquid, neither a solid nor a liquid, that splits into tiny fragments and reforms with ease and speed, reflecting the fluid magical quality of Hermes Mercurius.

As a planet, Mercury is the fastest moving of the planets close to the Earth. It is also quite elusive and hard to see as it is always in the same part of the sky as the Sun. Astrologically, Mercury is associated with speed of movement, mental agility, the element Air and most of all with communication.

Hermes Mercurius is a hermaphrodite, both male and female, a symbol of the Unity that fuses opposites into One, female with male, Yin with Yang. S/he represents our power to unite opposite forces and to create a bridge between the world of Spirit and the world of Matter, between the inner and the outer worlds, between the unconscious and the conscious, and our ability to heal separation and polarity and become whole.

In myth, Hermes Mercurius is the messenger of the gods, especially of Jupiter, and is able to travel between the worlds. S/he has wings on her feet and on her headdress to signify her transient nature and I think of her/m as an Angel being, a Spirit Guide or connecting link to the Spirit Realms. S/he is connected to the Earth, the planet of Matter, as well as the ethereal world of Spirit. S/he jumps through this interface between the worlds, the doorway that unites the many dimensions. S/he is known as the bringer of revelation, wisdom and the art of transformation.

Hermes Mercurius is also the Lord

of the Dead, who unites with the Lady of Life as one and the same energy. Through their Union there comes rebirth and reincarnation, never-ending cycles of Life on the path to self-realization.

Mercury has the added function of conducting the Souls of the Dead, as s/he walks between the worlds. Here there are similarities with the Christianized Archangel Michael.

In alchemy Hermes Mercurius is the great magician and healer, holding up the Caduceus as a symbol of our inherent power to unite and to heal. We are all great magicians and all great healers. We are all mutable transcendent beings, able to travel between Spirit and Matter and achieve transformation.

I activate my connection to Hermes Mercurius as part of myself and this opens me to the heart of the alchemy experience. I put my trust in myself and know for certain that I am able to transform myself and, through this, transform the world around me. By choosing to affirm and live as part of the whole, I experience the Oneness of all things and I belong to this Unity. It is here in my everyday life, here in the way that I relate to the world, here in the way I see myself as part of the Earth and her cycles and as the Elements, and here when I see myself as part of the great Web of Life.

The Wheel of the Year
&
the Alchemical Experiences

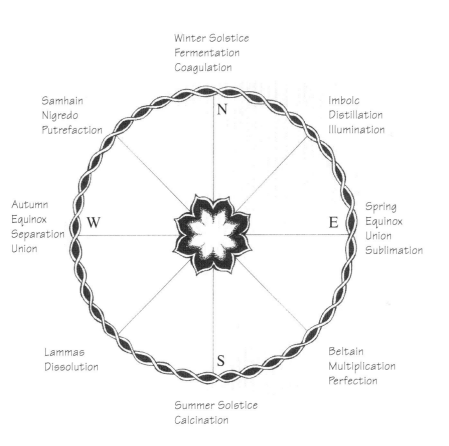

Winter Solstice
Fermentation
Coagulation

Samhain
Nigredo
Putrefaction

Imbolc
Distillation
Illumination

N

Autumn
Equinox
Separation
Union

W

E

Spring
Equinox
Union
Sublimation

Lammas
Dissolution

S

Beltain
Multiplication
Perfection

Summer Solstice
Calcination

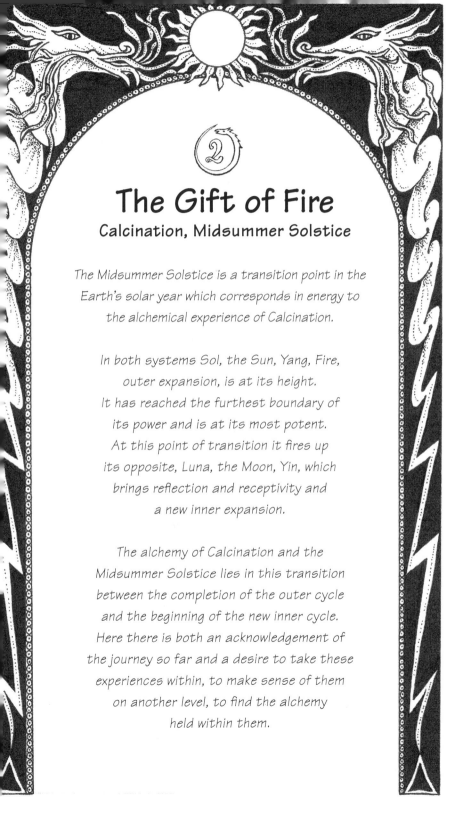

The Gift of Fire
Calcination, Midsummer Solstice

The Midsummer Solstice is a transition point in the Earth's solar year which corresponds in energy to the alchemical experience of Calcination.

*In both systems Sol, the Sun, Yang, Fire, outer expansion, is at its height.
It has reached the furthest boundary of its power and is at its most potent.
At this point of transition it fires up its opposite, Luna, the Moon, Yin, which brings reflection and receptivity and a new inner expansion.*

*The alchemy of Calcination and the Midsummer Solstice lies in this transition between the completion of the outer cycle and the beginning of the new inner cycle.
Here there is both an acknowledgement of the journey so far and a desire to take these experiences within, to make sense of them on another level, to find the alchemy held within them.*

The Alchemical Experience of Calcination

Calcination is the chemical reaction and alchemical metaphor that relates to the alchemist's use of Fire. Chemically, the Calcination process involves heating a substance in an open vessel until it is reduced to ashes. The alchemist uses the element Fire to consciously energize new paths forward, to burn away the things that are finished with and in doing so transforms their energy into an experience of the wisdom held within them.

Calcination is the alchemist's choice to activate the inner journey, and in this choice the ego and the will power become integrated with the desire for inner understanding and spiritual growth. Essentially, through this choice the ego begins a journey to transform itself, to transcend its limitations, attachments and boundaries, and to expand into the Limitless, the Infinite, Eternal Spirit.

The experience of Calcination, the alchemy of spiritual transformation, is symbolized by the Salamander, a mythical creature that lives in Fire. It thrives in it and revels in the transformation and change it creates. Other mythical Fire creatures are the Fire Dragon and the Phoenix, both symbols of transformation and rebirth. The Fire Dragon hatches from a golden egg and the phoenix rises from the ashes of the old.

Although the Calcination experience can be consciously chosen, it can also be thrust upon us through all of life's trials and tribulations, known as 'Trial by Fire'. Although not easy at the time, these are our life lessons, the growth experiences through which we learn and develop our spiritual awareness and inner wisdom. The ego is humbled in the process and this helps us to develop integrity.

Through Calcination our inner truth is tested and refined and our attachments and limitations are burned away, creating a death of an old way of being. At the heart of this experience is a rebirth into a new, more refined state and the forging of a connection to our deep inner wisdom.

The Calcination experience helps me to function in both the outer material world and the inner Spirit world at the same time. The more I jump into life's experiences, the more I embrace my potential to refine my spiritual understanding and live it as a natural part of my life. Through Calcination I am changed, transformed on the inside. I experience myself in a new and different way.

As I consciously choose to activate the inner journey, my rational mind lets go of its need to control and seeks to activate the alchemy of integration and connection to the Universal Flow. I become aware of what I wish to change or draw towards myself, and make new conscious intentions, establishing new patterns, new futures and new openings in my life.

The Alchemy of Fire

Fire is an energetic quality as well as a physical quality. It is a transformative force, creating action, energy and expansion. The dynamic and energetic use of Fire sets things in motion with commitment, boldness and passion.

I celebrate the living energy of Fire to generate energy, expansion and growth. It is the active power of response and release. Fire gets things moving and is a catalyst for change and transformation. Fire is associated with will power and conscious choice. Fire inspires me to take risks, to act on the strength of my convictions and to tap into my courage and inner strength. It lies in the spark of inspiration, the spark of the imagination, the inner spark of my Love and my passion and my desire for happiness. These are generated from within me and inspire my actions in the world.

As an alchemist, I seek Secret Fire, Hidden Fire or Sacred Fire, the Fire that lives within me and helps me to be in touch with what is truly important for my spiritual journey. I aim to unite my inner Fire with my outer Fire, so that everything I do in my everyday life, and in the world, is a reflection of this Union.

By uniting the two I create a doorway, an interface where my inner and outer Fire can fuse together. Their Union releases spontaneity and trust in myself, a clarity of inner strength and true integrity. I picture the opening this united Fire energy brings and jump right in. A new part of my journey has begun.

I fire up my commitment to my sacred journey. I use the energetic quality of Fire to fire up what I want to see happen or what to initiate or draw towards me. Fire is present in the things that I choose to do in my everyday life, what I set in motion by my actions, words and deeds.

I use Fire to activate my actions in the world. I feel empowered to release the wildfire of my Love and passion, to activate my commitment to help bring Peace and loving awareness into the world. I choose only to work with the loving, positive, life-enhancing solutions, to follow my 'Yes!', to trust my integrity and my intuition and to commit myself to openness and sharing. I feel the Fire grows strong in me as I choose to fire up the Love in my heart. It opens the doorway to my passion, to a place of trust in my power to be myself.

I use Fire to direct and open energy pathways, to activate my commitments, to set things in motion, to strengthen my intention, to activate my will power.

I light candles, incense, herbs or fires as symbolic acts, to mark beginnings, to activate my wishes and visions, to dedicate, to bring clarity and to energize. I use Fire to cleanse and purify, to burn away the old, the past, my limitations and anything that stops me from moving forwards or blocks my potential.

The Fire Dragon

In the symbolic language of alchemy, the Fire Dragon represents the essential energy of Fire. Dragons are part of our mythology and I seek to understand the Fire Dragon as an experience within myself. I have worked with Dragon energy many times over the years, especially Air Dragons and Earth Dragons, with which I have a natural affinity. But Fire Dragons are much more scary! They are volatile and unpredictable and can create chaos and total lack of control. There is always the danger of wildfire when Fire takes on its own momentum and a balanced and safe perspective can be up in flames and reduced to ashes in an instant. This is the fear that I must learn to transform as I become open to the lessons and the gifts of the Fire Dragon.

The Fire Dragon represents my passions, ecstasy, reckless ambition, uncontrollable emotional turmoil, intensity, sexuality, hilarity; it represents the edge of chaos, wildness and craziness. The Fire Dragon teaches me to embrace and accept these qualities and possibilities within myself as I embrace the other aspects of Fire energy such as positive action, clear direction, enthusiasm and creativity. All are born of daring, of taking risks, of jumping into Life. It is not always a safe place, but it is an exciting interface and a place of transition where alchemy happens.

I understand at a deep level that the Fire Dragon is

here to teach me to let go and trust, to hold nothing back. So I throw myself into the Dragon's Fire. I dare. I welcome the Fire that burns off my fear and anxieties, releasing these limitations to fuel my vital dance with Life. The Fire Dragon will always create change and transformation. This may create endings too, but I trust that there will always be new beginnings that will grow from this.

June 14th

The Phoenix

The Phoenix is the Firebird that rises from the ashes of the old, bringing inspiration from within and regeneration from the death of the old. It is a symbol of transformation and regeneration, sometimes called the Bird of Hermes or Mercury.

The Phoenix symbolizes the raising of consciousness to a higher form. As each of us strives to raise our consciousness, we contribute to the raising of spiritual consciousness on our planet, and huge transformational shifts are possible that will bring positive change to the world.

I want to be able to connect to the Phoenix energy within myself, so that I am connected to its essential energy with my heart as well as my mind. I decide to make an inner journey.

All is quiet out in the garden – just the gentle sounds of the birds – so I settle back comfortably in the deckchair and begin by focusing on my rhythmic breathing. When I become aware of thoughts, I gently send them floating down into the Earth. I keep breathing gently and slowly until I feel settled and still in myself and then I invite the Phoenix to come into my inner vision.

In my mind's eye a joyful, colourful, sparkling creature greets me! Red, orange and yellow light swirls around me and there are bubbles everywhere! My Firebird is exuberant, enthusiastic and fills me with delight and joy! I become aware that she is flying around an egg and this is her seed of joy. I understand this as the gift of new beginnings, the potential of transformation and regeneration. I also understand that this is the egg I also hold in this moment.

I ask the Firebird to take me on a journey and I climb onto her back. I am bathed in orange and red glowing light as we travel through one petal-shaped 'Vesica' opening after another. As soon as we go through one, there is another in front of us. We are inside a matrix of interconnecting openings, infinite space!

After a while I realize that I have come back to myself in my chair in the garden. I thank the Phoenix and sit a while musing on the understanding I have brought back. It is linked to being able to relax in the flow of Fire and to realizing that Fire creates a catalyst for the next thing to happen; Fire creates energy and movement, and movement helps me to interact with the natural flow of Life.

The Phoenix has helped me to contact my sense of trust in the continuing originality and spark of my Inner Fire. I feel I have shifted onto another level. I make a cup of tea and sit and sketch my Phoenix and the journey with the Phoenix to help remember this moment and internalize what I have learned.

The Alchemy of the Midsummer Solstice

The Midsummer Solstice falls between June 20th and 23rd in the Northern Hemisphere and between December 20th and 23rd in the Southern Hemisphere (see chart, page 27). The exact date and time of the Midsummer Solstice vary slightly each year. It is the longest day and shortest night of the year. This means that the outer cycle of the Sun has reached its height. The energy of Fire, Yang, has reached its full potential and now activates the new Yin cycle of the year.

From this point onwards the energy changes and the days will begin to shorten once again. Darkness will increase until the Yin cycle reaches its height at the Midwinter Solstice, the shortest day and longest night of the year, and activates a new Yang cycle once again.

Always the Earth is kept in balance in this way, with neither Light nor Dark being more or less important than the other. This harmony and equilibrium influences and is reflected in all Life on Earth.

The Midsummer Solstice, when Light activates the Dark, corresponds to the alchemical experience of Calcination. It is the same energy and I am able to understand Calcination better by uniting it with my understanding of the energy of the Midsummer Solstice. Midsummer Solstice is the height of the Sun's power, the height of Fire energy on the Earth and a great celebration of all that has been achieved during the Sun's waxing cycle. This is the end of its outer expansion and as always with endings, there are new beginnings. The Midsummer Solstice is a doorway into a new cycle and marks a transition, a change of energy. Here Fire activates the new Yin cycle, the inner growth cycle and the beginning of the influence of the element Water.

While it can feel significant to catch the precise moment of the Solstice, it is not always possible with the commitments of jobs or family life. I make a connection to the Solstice during the day or on the eve of the actual transition point by holding an awareness of the inherent alchemy of the Solstice and bringing it into all I do. I do something specific when I have the time to give it my full attention.

The Midsummer Solstice is a great doorway of transition and transformation. Before I step through, I celebrate my outer achievements, celebrate what I have brought into the world this year, celebrate what has blossomed and what I have manifested. As I step through this doorway I bring my outer achievements to the inside, so that I can continue to work with them as part of my inner journey.

I use the element of Fire to light introspection and insight, to activate my intuition, to look within and to bring a new perspective to my achievements. They become inspiration for my inner journey in the second half of the year, when I experience myself in a new and different way. This mirrors the alchemical experience of Calcination. This act of transformation doesn't happen in an instant at the Midsummer Solstice, but I use this festival to activate this alchemy, this shift in perception.

Many years ago I had the revelation that although for years I had celebrated the return of the Light at the Midwinter Solstice, I had never celebrated the return of the Dark at the Midsummer Solstice. This began a new journey for me, as I sought to balance the Dark and the Light within myself and to give equal value in my life to my inner world and my outer world.

Since then I have been developing and exploring my inner journey, the part of myself that receives impressions, feelings, intuition, insights and forms of communication that cannot be understood with the rational, logical mind. I am learning how to live my life in a way that includes and values the Dark, the inner world.

The Dark is good. It is a place for rest and renewal, the place of healing, wisdom and inner knowing. I use meditation, inner journeying and visualization to get in touch with this place within myself. I am developing my intuition, catching the receptive flashes of insight and messages that seem to jump out of nowhere and have become a natural way of life for me now. I have learned to trust myself. This has brought me a deep inner stability and inner Peace.

I connect to this place inside myself without fear. Fear disconnects me and fear distorts it. Every time I have the courage to turn and face my fears, I open the doors to healing the disconnection from my whole self.

Through my connection to the inner world I am increasingly aware of the changing flow of Time, how I can slip out of it and enter a rich multi-dimensional universe. Through my imagination I experience inner pathways and the wisdom of the Spirit Realms. For me this inner world is a benevolent world of Spirit Guides, Guardians, Angels, Nature Spirits and Elementals, and I am learning and developing new communication skills that are rich with exciting potential.

June 20th
The Summer Solstice

As usual at this time of year I am in Somerset, on the Glastonbury festival site. Most of my Solstices since the beginning of the 1980s have been spent here. I began as a festival-goer, got involved with the setting up of the Green Fields and became the co-ordinator of the Healing Area.

After a few years of doing this I wanted to have time to enjoy the whole festival again, so I passed on the coordinator's job and began to explore ways in which people could experience healing in other ways, apart from going to see a healer. This led to the creation of the Healing Area meditation and elemental gardens. These are places of beauty where festival-goers can step out of the hub of the busy festival and find a peaceful moment. They are lit up every night with nightlights and are a truly magical and healing experience.

This year I am helping to create a mandala, which is a circular pattern used as a focus for meditation and stilling the mind. We are making it from natural materials we find around the site, in the hedgerows and fields. These all have to be collected and stored ready for use before the festival-goers arrive. Over several days the materials are laid out on the ground in concentric rings, with an ever-expanding circumference. Each type of material creates a different ring of pattern, colour and texture. The finished mandala is 8 metres across and is a stunning celebration of the Earth.

We are on site early and are enjoying roaming the empty fields collecting materials. The Solstice has fallen five days before the festival starts and on Solstice Eve I take my usual Solstice walk to the Kings Meadow, the field right at the top of the site that has the stone circle in it now. It is such a beautiful field and tonight it is undisturbed by the crowds who will soon be flooding in here in their thousands.

There are just a handful of people sitting with the

stones, but I am pulled straight to the Kings Oak, the enormous old Oak tree there, an old friend of mine! I circle the tree, sensing the energy open for me to enter, and settle into a favourite seat on one of its huge roots that disappear from the trunk deep into the Earth.

I think about this interface between the upper and lower worlds of this glorious ancient Oak tree. There is as much of this tree below the ground as there is above the ground and it is perfectly balanced in 'the Above' and in 'the Below'. Its branches are visible in the light of the Sun and its roots invisible in the dark soil of the Earth. I think about the alchemist's maxim 'As Above, So Below' and I aim to be like the Oak tree, balanced between the world above and the world within. The more I am prepared to be open to my inner world and to explore my depths, the more stable I become, like a tree, more rooted in myself.

I reflect on what I have achieved this year on my journey. One by one I celebrate my achievements as well as acknowledging the things that haven't gone so well. I gather them all together and take each one inside myself, breathing them into myself and letting go of my attachment to them, knowing that this will transform them into my spiritual journey. I let them go, releasing them into my watery unconscious. Absurdly in my imagination I see each one bobbing about in a stream, like little coracles, happily dancing, swirling and spiralling down a river.

Drumming has started in the stone circle and I find

myself slipping in and out of Time, aware of the deep pulsing presence of this mighty Oak tree, aware of the interface between the worlds and the doorway of the Midsummer Solstice, this moment of transformation and transition, as one cycle ends and another begins.

I drift into a spontaneous daydream. In my daydream I am standing by a shallow river that is tumbling along in a gentle but busy manner. It gurgles over stones and the sounds become tunes in my head. I slip into the water and begin searching for a special stone. I find one that is smooth and a soft grey with white lines criss-crossing it. It fits really snugly in my hand and I feel pleased and immensely happy inside. I receive a message, like a voice in my head, to 'Follow what truly inspires you' and I follow the threads of understanding that this sparks in me.

I become aware of myself under the Kings Oak in the Kings Meadow again. I can hear someone playing a tin whistle a little way off. The drumming has stopped and there is a stillness and a feeling of timelessness. A Midsummer night's dream! I have to smile! I sit for a while, taking some conscious deep breaths, recounting my spontaneous daydream journey and anchoring myself firmly back into the field, the Oak and myself.

The Oak King gave me the message-gift to follow what truly inspires me, what is true for me, to trust my spirituality and to trust my integrity. I take this message into my heart, to light the Fire of my future actions.

I thank the Oak King wholeheartedly, sending a big wave of loving energy all around the tree like a big energy hug. I consciously merge my energy for a moment with the tree, taking its stable ancient energy inside myself, taking in the courage of Oak, the strength of it.

I find it hard to break the connection with the Oak and then I realize that I don't have to and I can carry it with me as I walk away, letting the energy slip away in its own good time. This feels so much better. My feet feel light and my heart is soaring as I walk back down the hill to find my friends and the campfire.

The Philosopher's Stone

The other gift of this inner dream-journey was the stone in the water. It feels important to grasp the significance of this. I relate it immediately to the Philosopher's Stone. A stone is, after all, a stone.

I understand the Philosopher's Stone as a place inside myself where I can store my insights as I gain and develop them at different stages of my journey. It is a connecting place, used to earth transient energy so that I can hold on to my insights and realizations and open doors to new levels of spiritual awareness and connection.

I can tap into the Stone, drawing upon its energy, at any time. The Stone is in me, I am the Stone, and it becomes more solid, more strengthened, with each layer of understanding that is added to it.

So I add to my Stone: 'Follow what truly inspires me.' To me this means following my heart and my Love, and this opens the way for the next part of my journey.

June 26th
The Hiroshima Peace Flame

In the bottom corner of the Kings Meadow is a large white dome that is being used as a focus for Peace. At its centre is the Hiroshima Peace Flame. This Flame was lit from the burning ruins of the Hiroshima atomic bomb dropped on Japan in 1945 and has been kept alight ever since as a symbol of Peace. Also called the Love Fire, it has been travelling around the world, kept alight and passed on amongst those who wish to help establish Peace in the world. It was brought to Glastonbury Festival by Hiroki Okano, a Japanese musician. (See Appendix, pages 267–8, for more details.)

The atmosphere in the Peace Dome is extraordinarily beautiful, a truly sacred space, filled with the Love of everyone who comes here to focus on Peace in the world and filled with many candles lit from the Love Fire. Every day there is meditation and ceremony, singing and toning, and every day hundreds of people at the festival send their Love and wish for Peace out into the world.

On the Saturday night we have a ceremony around the mandala and the Love Fire is brought down from the

Peace Dome to the Healing Area so that the children especially can light their candles from it. Hiroki tells its extraordinary story and everyone lights their candles and lanterns from the Peace Flame. We make a big circle of light around the mandala and send our Love and wish for Peace out into the world on a Cone of Power, blending all our notes into a beautiful harmony of energy. We light the mandala up with nightlights lit from the Peace Flame and it is wonderfully bright and energized with hope for the future.

I am so entranced by the alchemy of the Love Fire that I want to keep mine alight. But my candles will only burn for six hours! So keeping the Flame alight becomes an important focus of my day and my night. Each time I light a new candle from the wick of the old one, I make an invocation for Peace. It is a powerful thing to do and the Peace and the Love in my heart are fired up with each new invocation.

After I have transported the Peace Flame home, a friend brings me some 24-hour candles and some three-day candles and I can have a full night's sleep again! Friends come and share the Flame and it continues on its way to other festivals and Peace Groups.

It becomes the focus for my daily meditation and my understanding of Peace. My understanding of the transformative power of Love becomes deeper and more powerful every day. It is an extraordinary journey. I begin to see that Peace begins and grows in our hearts and it is this that will bring Peace into the world.

Eventually my partner has the idea that we can light the pilot light of our central heating system with the Peace Flame, as this never goes out, and so the alchemy continues and I like to think our house is fired up with Love and Peace every day!

July 1st
A Day of Fire Alchemy

I decide to take some time to connect to myself in a meditative way and to see what comes from within. Gardening always helps me do this, or walking in the woods, but today I am drawn to a part of my garden in which I have created outdoor celebration shrines to each of the Five Elements.

Each element faces the traditional direction for the Celtic/Northern European system, as this is my heritage. Air faces the East, Fire faces the South, Water faces the West, Earth faces the North and Spirit is at the centre of the circle and present in all the other elements around the circle. In each direction I have plants that reflect the colours and energy of each of the Five Elements, and have included things that help to mark them and make an energetic connection for me.

Today I decide to re-create the Fire shrine area. There are remnants of things there that I planted previously. The stunning bright red Bergamot flowers are in flower now, and the Blackcurrant Sage with its mass of magenta flowers. Magenta is the colour of spiritual Fire, as it combines the red of Fire with the purple of Spirit. There is also a rough pile of stones left over from a small ritual cairn I made at the Midsummer Solstice last year. Each stone represented something that I wanted to fire up consciously in my life. Often over this last year I've sat in the garden and remembered my Fire cairn stones and what they represented: to meditate every day; to let go of worry; to transform resentments and fears into trust and Love; to act on my intuition; to become more spontaneous; to find key triggers to use so that I am less controlling; and to remember to see the funny side of life. Each one of these has had an influence on my year's journey and now I sit for a while and reflect on the joys and inspiration that each one has brought me. I take them all inside myself, knowing that I will continue to grow with them. I decide not to change any of them, but to find deeper levels of understanding in them, to root them ever more firmly into my life.

I make a ring with the Fire cairn stones, adding a few more to make a small Fire circle to use for lighting small ritual fires. It is only about 10 centimetres across, so it can take small twigs and can also be used as a place to put nightlights.

This immediately brings up the question of what I wish to do now in this ritual Fire circle. I keep focused on this as I continue to clear the rest of the area. I hang small mirrors and crystals in the Hawthorn tree to catch the light and the Sun. I dig up and replant some Nasturtiums and Calendula plants that have reseeded in the vegetable garden and will bring a lot of fiery reds, yellows and oranges later on in the year. I lay lengths of slate radiating out from all around the Fire circle, which gives the whole thing a feeling of expansion. It all looks wonderful and I feel ready to play with Fire!

I light a candle from the Peace Flame and bring it out to the Fire circle, saying:

'I dedicate this Fire circle to the energy of Fire!
To the expansion of Love and of Peace! Love Fire!
The Spark of Life! To my commitment to change and
transformation within myself and in the world!
To the transference of energy from the inside to the
outside! To my imagination! To spontaneity!
To the spark of Inspiration! To creativity!
To Vision! Choice! Laughter! Joy! Action! Liberation!
Courage! Release! To the Spirit of Calcination, the
transference of energy from the outside to the inside!'

I gather twigs and dead leaves from around the garden as I focus on the alchemy of the Calcination experience. These twigs represent the year gone by, the past. I place these in my ritual Fire circle. I then write on pieces of paper what I wish to transform in the Fire, what I wish to release, to leave behind in the old cycle and to take inside myself and transform during the new inner reflective cycle.

I write: 'Feeling small', 'Lack of confidence', 'Feeling disempowered', 'Not acting on my intuition or saying what I think for fear of rejection.' I poke these bits of paper in amongst the sticks.

Then I write some new Fire intentions, the things that I wish to energize. I write: 'To choose what I wish to give energy to', ' To become an alchemist of the heart', ' To help the Earth', 'To work for Peace and Love in the world' and poke these in too.

Then I set fire to them all, using the flame of the Love Fire, and watch as the flames gobble up my offerings until there is just a small pile of ash left. The ashes of Calcination!

My affection for Fire is beginning to deepen. I reflect on how Fire is the initiator of change and transformation through the alchemy of our intention and focus. My commitment to my aims brings the spark of Life to them, sets them in motion. Giving attention to them strengthens them, sets them alight. My conscious choice is to fire up loving and positive energy so that this is what I will attract and this is what will expand.

The Power of my 'Yes!'

Committing to the power of my 'Yes!' is an act of Fire alchemy. The energy of 'Yes' opens the energy doorways. Similarly, the energy of 'No' will close off a pathway. I may be closing or opening pathways without realizing it. As an alchemist I am aiming to work with energy in a conscious way, to activate and open that which I wish to draw towards myself and to close off that which I no longer wish to influence me and my life. I seek a place in myself where I neither need nor seek approval from others. I take my power and live the life that I want to live. I commit myself with courage and determination to create positive changes. I put into action anything that might bring my goals closer and then lovingly release any attachment I might have to them. It is important that I keep my messages clear and loving and also that I release my attachment to the outcome. I release any hold that my longing and hopes may have over me.

Whatever I choose to direct my actions, words and deeds towards is what I strengthen and draw towards myself. Choosing to work with the transformative power of Universal Love will ensure that I draw healing and positive transformation towards myself. Giving and receiving are inextricably linked, each informs the other and creates open channels for the energy to travel along.

I remember, whenever I can, that I am open to miracles happening, and that being open to this keeps the energy of all possibilities flowing and connected.

HERMES MERCURIUS

Hermes Mercurius is a key inspiration on my journey into alchemy and I seek to understand each of the alchemical experiences and my use of the Five Elements through her/m. S/he is outside me and inside me, a symbol of Unity as well as a symbol of my potential to be this Unity.

I light a Love Fire candle from the Peace Flame pilot light and dedicate the Flame to my journey with the Spirit of Hermes Mercurius. This fires up the connection and I stare into the flame as I consciously meditate on the energy of Hermes Mercurius and see where this takes me.

Hermes Mercurius holds up the Caduceus, the symbol of integrated power of balance and healing. S/he has mastered all the Five Elements and is able to use their qualities with harmony and balance. All are blended within her/m and so within me.

The wings on her feet and the wings on her head represent her swiftness, her ability to transcend Time and Space and slip in and out of the Matrix at will.

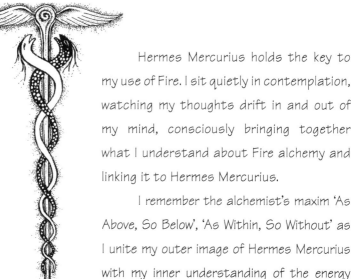

Hermes Mercurius holds the key to my use of Fire. I sit quietly in contemplation, watching my thoughts drift in and out of my mind, consciously bringing together what I understand about Fire alchemy and linking it to Hermes Mercurius.

I remember the alchemist's maxim 'As Above, So Below', 'As Within, So Without' as I unite my outer image of Hermes Mercurius with my inner understanding of the energy she represents, in myth, in alchemy and in me.

I receive an image of fleeting energy that moves like wildfire, uncontained and free. It is Hermes Mercurius as the Spirit of Quicksilver. S/he moves quickly, just as Fire does! There is no time to think!

I am being asked to trust that my Fire is the catalyst for change and transformation, to jump into Life with boldness and certainty. I know that I can trust the Fire that comes from within, my spiritual Fire, the alchemist's Secret Fire. I find this in my heart, in the things that move me to express my Love and in the Love that inspires me to action. I let this fly, knowing it is the flame of healing and loving transformation. When I trust my Love Fire,

I trust each doorway that opens, trust my spontaneity, trust my words, trust my actions and trust the Fire that I release. This is my freedom and this is my inner Fire, my ability to live in the moment and be a catalyst for transformation and healing.

I thank Hermes Mercurius for this vision and as I jump into the next part of the cycle I fire up my inner path and the path of the heart.

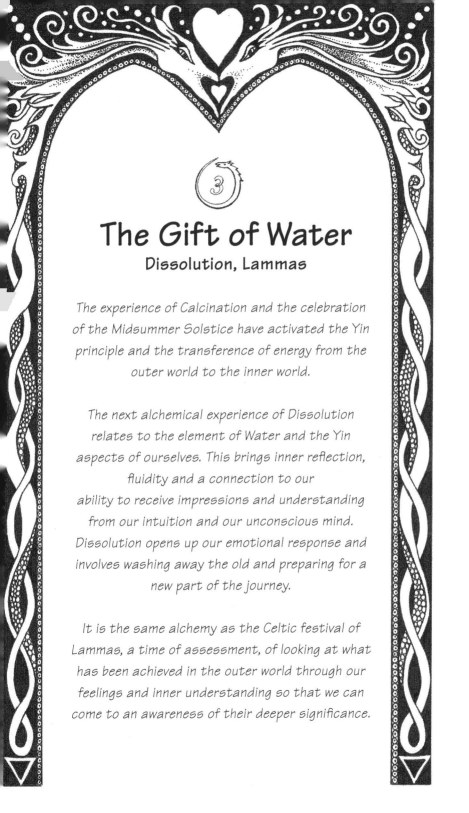

3

The Gift of Water
Dissolution, Lammas

The experience of Calcination and the celebration of the Midsummer Solstice have activated the Yin principle and the transference of energy from the outer world to the inner world.

The next alchemical experience of Dissolution relates to the element of Water and the Yin aspects of ourselves. This brings inner reflection, fluidity and a connection to our ability to receive impressions and understanding from our intuition and our unconscious mind. Dissolution opens up our emotional response and involves washing away the old and preparing for a new part of the journey.

It is the same alchemy as the Celtic festival of Lammas, a time of assessment, of looking at what has been achieved in the outer world through our feelings and inner understanding so that we can come to an awareness of their deeper significance.

The Alchemical Experience of Dissolution

Dissolution relates to the energetic use of Water. Chemically, the ashes and any other residues from the Fire of Calcination are put into the alchemical vessel and dissolved in water. Alchemically, all that has been achieved on the surface, out in the light, under the Sun, is released into the watery unconscious. This is the alchemical transference of Sol consciousness into Luna consciousness, the transformation of Fire into Water.

The Dissolution experience encourages us to release our emotions, but first we have to fully engage with what we are feeling. Once we acknowledge our emotions we are able to take the next step and release our attachment to them and move on. Then we are able to move through any negative energy we may be creating into a more positive place.

Emotion is energy in motion, the energy of flow and movement that keeps us healthy and affects every cell in our bodies.

Through the experience of Dissolution I take my achievements within, to feel them and to understand them not with my rational mind, but with an intuitive inner knowing. The quest for Truth begins with Dissolution. I ask, 'How do my achievements help my inner journey, my spiritual journey?'

Dissolution helps me to connect to my inner way of knowing so that I do what feels right in my heart and Soul.

My inner morality, conscience and integrity resonate with my ever-deepening understanding that everything I do, say or even think affects someone somewhere and eventually returns to me.

By my experiences, by my mistakes, I learn and grow in understanding. How I transform my mistakes is at the heart of the Dissolution experience. If I blame other people for them I remain caught up in them, becoming stuck in resentment and pain. I turn inwards, multiplying resentment and blame and blocking the energy of transformation. If I bury and ignore them they are wasted, like seeds falling onto concrete, and the opportunities for inner growth and healing are lost. If they are consciously picked up, looked at courageously, with Love, then they have Life and movement and hold new seeds and new growth for the future.

Water and the Dissolution experience teach me to keep flowing, not to become stuck, so when I am full of painful remorse for the hurt I may have caused others, I can release myself from the negativity of guilt and move on. I do this by opening my heart and sending out Unconditional Love, forgiveness and compassion to myself, to those who I hurt and to those who have hurt me. This alchemy opens the doorway to the powerful transformative power of Love. The healing flow of Universal Love is a cleansing process that clears away the fears and hurts that are locked inside us and perpetuate the pain. Love is the catalyst that brings healing to the past, the present and the future.

I use the Dissolution process to dissolve rigid attitudes, to let go of old beliefs and separatist thinking, the us and them' mentality and the old way of 'blame and separate'. I am open to the alchemical path of 'unite and heal' as I open myself to the Infinite Flow of Universal Love at my core. I know that healing begins here and now, in this moment, with me.

The Alchemy of Water

I celebrate Water as the Bringer of Life', a connecti force, a flowing and joining force circulating round our planet and our bodies, constantly on the move, regenerating and re-creating itself.

Our physical bodies are largely made up of water. The water inside each of us connects us to all Life, to the past and to the future. It may have come from the stars. It has been in the clouds, in the rain, in the snow-capped mountains, the mountain streams, the mighty rivers and vast oceans and seas of the Earth. The spring water that I drink has come from deep within the Earth. It has been filtered and cleansed by the rocks and has absorbed minerals and the quality and energy of Life on its journey.

Water is always changing yet always remains the same. It has the ability to mutate between liquid, gaseous and solid forms, becoming ice and steam, fog and mist. It has many moods, from the still pool to the mighty storm waves.

What happens to water when it becomes stagnant and isolated? It turns in on itself and becomes unhealthy. Water needs to keep flowing and connecting. This gives it Life. As it swirls and eddies it becomes self-cleaning, self-regulating and self-revitalizing. As we ourselves are water, there is much we can learn from the natural alchemy of water.

Water has hidden depths and hidden talents. It has a memory and will hold an imprint of whatever thought or substance it receives. It can be blessed and changes because of this. It is used in baptism, a sacred alchemical act. It can be used for healing, to clear the past and initiate a new beginning, for any act of dedication, for clearing energy and for creating connection and integration. This is its alchemy.

The unique electrochemical properties of water allow it to hold the memory of any substance that it has held in an energetic suspension. This is the principle of homoeopathy, where substances are shaken vigorously to 'potentize' them and then diluted beyond a level where science can measure that any substance is present. These highly diluted potencies are very effective medicine, as all those who use them will testify. They work by activating the body to heal itself, stimulating the Life Force to create movement and flow once again.

Water represents the Yin, the receptive principle. It helps me to unlock the hidden parts of myself. To do this I have to open myself to receptivity, to my connection to the Universal Flow. To receive is equally important as to act. When I open myself to receive, I receive healing, I receive flashes of insight and inspiration, I receive intuitive impressions, I receive energy and feelings both from myself and from other people.

My watery nature is the world within, the world of my inner feelings, my flowing emotions and my deep inner knowing. It is uncharted territory, the hidden parts of my self, the Inner Realms, the Dark, formless, flowing Infinity, waiting to receive whatever I bring to it.

The Alchemy of Lammas

The Celtic festival of Lammas falls around the end of July/beginning of August in the Northern Hemisphere and the end of January/beginning of February in the Southern Hemisphere (see chart on page 27). Lammas celebrates the power of the Sun and Water, the fulfilment of our outer activities, and is the first recognition of our harvest. The alchemy of Lammas lies in the transference of Fire into Water, Yang into Yin, bringing transformation and change to our awareness.

Lammas marks the gathering in of the grain harvest, the celebration of the seed that will feed us through the winter months and also of the seed that will lie dormant during the winter and be grown the next spring to provide us with the following year's harvest. It is a reminder to honour and give thanks for the gifts from the Earth, to bless the food that is grown and eaten.

Like the experience of Dissolution, Lammas celebrates the alchemy of Fire and Water. At this time there is still energy in the Sun to ripen the crops, yet rain is also needed to swell the seeds and the fruit. In the past cooking fires were honoured at Lammas, and beer, wine, cider and whiskey were drunk, celebrating the transformative power of Fire and Water.

Lammas was also a time of fairs and tribal gatherings. In the north of England these were known as 'the Wakes', thereby bringing an awareness of the dying year, the death of the Sun and the turning inward to a deeper understanding of our year's cycle.

The Celtic god Lugh or Lug, a Sun King, gives up his power at Lammas. He represents the Sun surrendering to the waning cycle. We too must sacrifice our outer selves and the outer energy of the year and welcome the inner journey. This is crucial to our well-being. Here at Lammas we take our awareness within, into our watery Inner Realms, to understand ourselves in a different way.

Lammas is traditionally a time for assessment, as is the experience of Dissolution. At this time I become receptive to my feelings and to the insights they bring to my inner journey. Lammas assessment calls for complete honesty and the courage to face myself. I look at my difficulties, my downfalls, my crisis points, and I value them for the lessons they bring me. I also value and celebrate my high points, joys and moments of perfection. My experiences show me who I am at this point in time and my own assessment of my journey helps me see my path forward. For me, my heart and my Love lead the way. I assess my experiences through how much Love I gave or didn't give, for in this lies the catalyst to transformation from within.

As the Sun transforms the seeds within the harvest, I too am able to transform my experiences into new seeds for the future. Lammas assessment helps me to gather the seeds of new directions that I will take with me into the dark of the year. This is the alchemy of Lammas.

The main alchemical symbols for Dissolution and Lammas are the Sea Serpent, the Mermaid, the Mirror, the Moon and the Chalice. They are all symbols of reflection, purification and hidden wisdom, and hold the key to the qualities of our watery unconscious. Other symbols include the many aspects of Water: spirals, eddies, waves, rivers or streams, fountains, wells, springs, clouds, ice, steam and rain. Boats symbolize safe passage and the inner journey.

July 4th
The Chalice Meditation

I sit quietly and comfortably in my room this morning, with the window open to the sounds and smells of the day.

It is warm but raining steadily. The garden is so green and lush, very overgrown and exotic!

I begin with a meditation, beginning as always with deep breathing, keeping focused on my breath, slowing it down, filling my lungs, filling myself with this moment. I become lost in the sound of the rain falling and my lungs and body responding to the increase of breath.

I feel myself sinking through layers, sinking deeper and deeper into a state of stillness. I consciously connect to my Heart chakra, in the centre of my chest, and picture it as a beautiful Chalice. This is my alchemist's vessel or flask, the place inside me where the alchemy happens. Today I am open to experience the alchemy of Dissolution, transferring my energy from without to within. This means connecting to my feelings and the wisdom of Universal Love.

I open myself to feelings of Universal Love and intense happiness by remembering the things and the people that make me happy. I open myself to this happiness and let it wash over me. It fills my Heart chakra and my Chalice with Love until it becomes so full it overflows. I radiate joy, sending it out all around my body, to each of my chakras in turn, feeling myself fluid and connected on all levels. When the power of the joy begins to recede, I return to the original thoughts and refill my Chalice to overflowing again.

Then I send this joy and happiness outwards, to my family, to my friends, to the people I know who need some joy and healing. I send it out into the world to those who are suffering and in despair.

I slowly let the connections fade and rest, and I sit for a while, back in my centre, my still place, just sitting and being', listening to the rain again.

I am struck by the cyclic nature of this kind of alchemy. It is not a one-way exchange. As I give out, I am filled up — I am filled with a calm joy, a presence of Unity and Oneness, a compassionate, loving, healing energy that is not bound by me, or by Time, or by Space. This is my Dissolution experience.

July 27th
Messages from Water

Nothing about Water is rational. It invites us to challenge our reliance on rational thinking, to explore other parts of ourselves, other ways of understanding.

Japanese scientist Masaru Emoto was able to photograph the beautiful ice crystals revealed under the microscope when he froze spring water. These revealed hexagonal patterns and six-pointed star shapes full of light and Life. These photographs show that each and every crystal, like our fingerprints, is unique and different from the next.

Masaru Emoto's remarkable book The Message from Water shows many photographs of ice crystals taken from all around the world. The tap-water samples taken from our major cities reveal shockingly dark, ugly and grotesque shapes and are enough to put me off drinking tap water.

Another set of photos, taken before and after a priest offered healing prayers for one hour by a dam in Japan, shows the awesome transformation of the dam-water crystals from dark and chaotic shapes to beautiful complex six-pointed stars of light.

Masaru Emoto's photographs show that our words, our prayers, our Love and our energy have the power to change water. He also placed different words on jars of spring water and photographed the astonishing changes in the patterns of the water crystals that resulted. Negative words produced ugly formless dull shapes, and positive, loving words created complex six-pointed stars and hexagons of light and beauty. The water responded to thedifferent vibrations of the different words and the emotional response of humans to the different words.

It does not take a huge leap of imagination to see how we influence each other and each other's health through the power of our words and thoughts, loving or otherwise. So I aim to become more consciously aware of what energy I am sending out with my words, thoughts and emotions. I bless the food I eat and the water I drink and effectively change what I take into my body. The water becomes transmuted and energized by what I bring to it. When I give thanks for its Life-giving qualities, the Life-giving qualities increase.

Love and appreciation create a different quality of food and water, increasing their ability to cleanse, heal and energize our cells.

This offers huge potential for healing both ourselves and the polluted waters of the Earth. I am particularly inspired by our potential to change tap water and each time I fill the water filter from the tap, I envelop the jug in a brilliant wave of Love-light. I do the same again before I use it. If one man can transform a whole dam of water in one hour, then surely I can transform this small jug full of water in a few seconds! I am willing to trust that I have done it.

This is the kind of alchemy we can all do to consciously increase health and well-being. For what we send out we also receive ourselves.

August 6th
Rainbows and Reflection

Today is Hiroshima Day and I light lots of candles from the Peace Flame, still alchemically held in the centralheating pilot light. I reflect on Peace in the world and the great turning of the tide that has begun as the world connects to a more wholesome spirituality. I send Universal Love and the Spirit of Unity out into the world, envisioning the great oceans' tides turning and Love, Unity and inner Peace rolling onto the shores bringing a change of heart, a reconnection to the joy of sharing and giving, to basic human kindness as a force for change and transformation in the world.

I pour a glass of spring water and sit cradling it in my hands, letting myself feel a deep connection to the Spirit of Water. I thank the water for its power of transformation and its power of healing. I slowly move my hands in a circular motion over it. While I am doing this I imagine beautiful rainbow light flowing from my hands into the water. A rainbow of hope for our Earth! Peace and harmony in our hearts!

I focus on the alchemy of Dissolution and Lammas, sitting quietly for a while, simply relaxing and being open to my thoughts and feelings, to impressions I receive from myself. I am not trying to think, not trying to get anywhere or to come to any conclusions. I am simply being in the moment.

I connect to each of the Five Elements in turn, drawing them around me in a circle and drawing them inside myself like good friends I am glad to see. I take each element into my heart, so that I feel its presence within me, as part of my body and part of my internal understanding of its alchemy.

I reflect on where this journey is leading me. I ask myself, 'What am I aware of harvesting at this time and what are the seeds inherent in my harvest? What do I need to transform with Unconditional Love? What do I need to let go of? What do I want to nurture?'

I give myself some time to muse on these questions while sitting peacefully, relaxing and being receptive to my feelings. I notice what I am feeling about different aspects of my harvest and pour Love into the experiences that I have found difficult and revealing.

Then I let go of the need to complete everything at once, to judge or to blame others or myself. Everything is part of a process and everything is unfolding. I trust that what I have set in motion by my Love will bear fruit in time in its own unique way. I do not need to control it, just sow the seeds for the alchemy to begin.

I drink the rainbow-charged water and take in the infusion of rainbow light, the Spirit of hope, of harmony and Peace. I resolve to do this often, to activate the energy of the rainbow and also to infuse water in other ways.

I fill a glass with spring water and leave it outside to charge up in the light of the Moon. This will create another alchemical infusion that I can drink.

Luna Consciousness

The Moon, Luna, has a special place in alchemy as equal partner to the Sun. In the Celtic system too, the Sun and the Moon, represented by the elements Fire and Water, are honoured and respected as equal parts of the whole. Luna alchemy brings reconnection to our deep inner selves and our creativity. Luna consciousness is the intelligence of the heart, inner wisdom and our ability to tap into and be guided by our emotional responses, our intuition and inner wisdom.

Luna consciousness reminds me of the place inside myself that is beyond words. It invites me to listen and to be receptive. I remember that I am always part of the whole, resonating with all the unseen energy patterns flowing around me all the time. I receive positive or negative energy, good or ill will, whatever is directed my way. I can't see this but I do feel it at a subtle level. It can influence how I am feeling, adding to my health and well-being or making me vulnerable to illness. By the same token other people will receive the energy I send to them. I am aware of my responsibility for this with every thought about other people that I have.

Full Moon Alchemy

The Full Moon has a considerable influence on the growth of plants and on reproduction cycles and it pulls on all the water on the planet, including the water in our bodies. We all feel its influence, whether we are conscious of it or not.

The Full Moon brings connection to my instinctual wisdom and my intuition. It brings release from within and I use it to release my emotions, my poetry, my songs and artwork. This helps me to tap into ancestral memory and make conscious the unconscious.

I use the alchemy of the Full Moon to energize new pathways, to activate Love and other emotions, to reveal what is hidden and to tap into my psychic abilities, which are heightened at this time.

I also use the Full Moon to honour anything that has been brought to culmination, completion and fruition, and to take it to another stage of its development, to take it inwards with the waning cycle of the Moon.

Full Moon Elixirs

I create alchemical infusions by putting crystals in spring water and leaving them out in the Full Moon to charge them up with Luna energy. The water is then infused with the qualities of the crystal and the qualities of the Moon and becomes an elixir. For anyone interested in working with crystals, this is an interesting alchemy to explore.

Whatever emotional energy I bring to the water when making an elixir also adds to its alchemy. I infuse my elixirs with Unconditional Love, with Oneness of Spirit, and this too becomes part of their healing energy.

New Moon or Dark Moon Alchemy

When the Moon is New, or Dark, its energy influences new beginnings. It is like a seed waiting to grow, a pause before rebirth.

I use this time for planting seeds of ideas, seeds of vision, seeds of daring, seeds of hope. The New Moon sets things in motion and I use it to begin new projects, to make new resolutions, affirmations or statements of intention.

August 24th
The Alchemy of Fire and Water

I wake early this morning to a clear blue sky and the promise of a beautiful sunny day. I am out early in the garden and once again I am drawn to the Chamomile beds. This has happened for several days and now I take notice of it and decide to do something about it. The conditions are perfect for making flower essences, so I go and get a glass bowl and some spring water.

Flower remedies hold the healing imprint of flowers that have lain on water in the sunshine. They impart their healing qualities into the water, which then becomes a concentration of the healing essences of the plant. These act on the emotions to stimulate change in the subtle energy of the body and this leads to physical healing.

I sit near the plants for a while, enjoying their simple perfection. Their energy is dreamy and meditative, bringing me a feeling of inner calm and stillness. This is the essential energy of Chamomile that I am preserving for future use. I place a glass bowl of spring water under the plants and with Love and gratitude to the Sprit of Chamomile, I nip off some of the flowers and let them fall face down in the water. (Flower essences can also be made without the actual plant being in the water.)

I leave the bowl in the sunshine amongst the Chamomile plants, and sit with it a while, enjoying how good it looks twinkling there in the sunlight and how good I am feeling to be fully engaged with Chamomile at last. Making the flower essence means that I will be able to connect to Chamomile whenever I need its peaceful presence again, even in the middle of the winter. This moment, this morning with the Chamomile, this Love, will live on and become part of the flower essence I am making. This is the alchemy. The water will hold the memory not only of the plants' essence and Spirit, but also the essence of Love that I have brought to the process.

When I am making essences I sit near the plants and write down any thoughts that come to me, snatches of poetry and musings, thoughts that surface about how this plant makes me feel. I also draw the plant. Not how it looks necessarily, but again from my sensing of its essential energy.

After a while, when I feel it is ready, I remove the flowerheads of the Chamomile and, with gratitude and Love to the plants, to the Water and to the sunshine, I take a drink of the infusion. I take in the simple alchemy, the healing, the gift of the Chamomile, the energy of Water and the Sun. I am so glad I made the time for this experience today. I raise the bowl in a toast to the Chamomile plants, a toast to the alchemy of Sun and Water and a toast to myself. I honour this delightful moment and drink. I then give some of the infused water to the plant with my Love and thanks.

Flower essences need to be preserved so that we can use them when we need them, so I clean a jam jar and lid in preparation. I remove the flower petals from the water with a twig, and then half fill the jar with the infused spring water.

The rest of the jar is filled up with brandy. I use acrylics to paint the name of each flower on the relevant jar. The jars should be of dark glass to preserve the essences effectively, so I have an enjoyable time sitting in the sunshine wrapping the jar in dark material and threads. This is the 'mother tincture' and will be decanted into small dropper bottles to use when needed, usually four drops at a time with water, three times a day.

Making flower essences help me to use my intuition. I use them for as long as I feel I need to and stop when I feel their influence has created a shift at an emotional level and I no longer need them. When I take flower essences, even if I have not made them personally, I create an energetic connection to the plant or tree species at the same time, either physically or by picturing the plant in my mind's eye.

I have many lovely images in my mind's eye from today and it has been a great joy to be here in the garden connecting intuitively to the plants I have nurtured and Love.

August 27th
A Vision Quest

I decide to have a vision quest day, a day for reflection and reconnection to my inner self, a day that supports my quest for inner Peace, a day spent in Nature, on my own, focused on my Dissolution experience.

I have been thinking of a special spring I love to visit, where the water pours out of a hole from deep in the hillside. It has a special 'otherworldly' energy, full of the sounds and Spirits of Water.

Before I go to bed I meditate and try to empty my mind of any preconceived ideas about what tomorrow will bring, so that I am open to the flow and to guidance from within.

I wake at 5 o'clock, as I often do. The light is clear and bright. I am excited by the prospect of a whole day to myself and I am up, drinking tea in the garden by 5.15. I love being outside in the early morning light. It is my favourite time of the day. Everything is so fresh and new, bursting with the energy of Life and expectancy.

I gather some flowers from the garden to take to the spring. Thinking of the old practice of throwing in offerings to give thanks to the Spirits of Water, I put a small pottery Moon woman that I made into my pocket. I take with me a bottle of spring water, some dried fruit, a bag of nuts, some apples and a notebook and pen.

Unfortunately, I have to drive to get to the spring, but there is very little on the roads at this time of day and I am soon off the main roads and onto the back lanes. I park in the nearest little car park to the spring and sit by the river for a while, enjoying the early morning sunshine, daydreaming, drifting, watching the birds and the twinkling light in the trees and on the water and listening to the song of the river. I gather myself together and at the same time extend myself to touch and receive the Spirits of this place, the trees and the plants and all of Nature here in this moment. I feel alive and vibrant! A deep calm descends upon me. I am so glad to be here and so early in the morning! I am in a state of alert receptivity, open to what the day will reveal.

I cross the river by the stepping stones and walk slowly up through the woods, drinking in the atmosphere, keeping myself in a meditative state with all my senses open but all my thoughts shut down. The fast-flowing stream is always beside me, busy on its way down the hillside, gushing over rocks and stones to become the river at the bottom of the valley. As I walk along I sing myself into harmony with the stream and sing myself into a deeper meditation and Oneness with the landscape all around me.

When I reach the spring I sit for a long while on a rock near where the water gushes out of the spring pool, falling over the edge to become the stream I have just followed. As always when I am here, the sound of the water lulls me into a meditative state. All thoughts are gone. I am simply One with the moment, with the Spirit of this place and with the landscape around me. It is a feeling of melting, of merging, of Union. Time seems to stand still and I am filled with such calm, such inner Peace and such contented fullness.

After a while I realize what I want to do here today. One by one I toss the flowers I have brought into the water, each time naming what I am releasing with Love and compassion. I forgive myself, I forgive others, and I let go of all my turmoil and anxiety, my anger, my self-righteousness. I let it all go with each flower I toss in the water, see it rushing off down the stream, cleansed by my Love, cleansed by the water, carried off to eventually become part of the great ocean. I free myself of all my anxieties, my sadness, my worries, all the mistakes I made – all the things that have been preying on my mind, dampening my Fire and disconnecting me from my generous loving nature. I let them all go. Now I am free to begin again with a fresh focus of healing and Love.

It doesn't matter if I have to do this letting go process again and again. Each time I do it, it strengthens my connection to the alchemy and transformative power of Universal Love. I hope that I can hold on to this great Love that I am feeling now. I remember my Philosopher's Stone inside me and I earth the Love I am feeling now and store it inside my Stone so that I can connect to it and use it again whenever I need to.

I sit for a long time after my flowers have rushed off down the stream. I am so thankful for this moment and this place and for being able to do these transformative rituals that help me to connect to myself in this special way. I am actively engaged in the process of change now and I am creating change from the inside. I celebrate this shift in focus and the journey that leads me to explore the subtle energy that lies all around me and within me.

A piece of yellow sandstone seems to wink at me from the water and I take it out and see that it is a rough egg shape.

It feels like a gift from the place, a connector that I can use whenever I wish to return here in my mind's eye or return inside myself to link to the energy that I have experienced today. I thank the stone for giving itself to me and promise I will return it to this place when I no longer need it.

I take off my shoes and socks and get into the icy water, splashing it over myself, feeling its intensity and its Life. It's glorious and magical to be here! Simple and powerful! A moment of pure perfection!

After this I eat to ground my energy, drink some spring water and sit and enjoy the vibrant magic of this very special place.

Before I leave I remember my pottery Moon woman. I thought I would throw her into the opening of the spring, but instead I am drawn to put her in the dark black earth near the spring. Covering her over with leaves, I thank the Spirits of the spring, the Spirits of Water and the Spirits of the place, and head off back down the hill through the woods to reconnect to the everyday world once again.

HERMES MERCURIUS

My ongoing relationship with Hermes Mercurius awakens my ability to use my intuition and my feeling mind, to go beyond the surface reality and to change my perceptions. S/he is here in the Dissolution experience, inviting me to open a door to my inner self and my inner way of knowing.

When I take the time to reconnect to my inner world, I feel a sense of rightness, of coming home, of being back on track. I trust this inner way of knowing, I trust myself to follow what feels right. As I give it more importance in my life, my actions, my words and my thoughts are becoming naturally informed by my intuition and my sixth sense. I am more aware of receiving telepathic communication, and many synchronicities happen, which increasingly adds to the feeling that I am in the right place at the right time.

Through Hermes Mercurius I am developing new skills that increase my understanding of other levels of communication, levels that lie beneath the surface in the watery depths. This is a creative, intuitive place of receptive

awareness that I am open to act from.

I make myself comfortable and state my intention to journey to make a connection to Hermes Mercurius. I begin by breathing deeply and letting my energy settle to the Earth. I then visualize everything that Hermes Mercurius represents to me, so that I reach out into my imagination and touch her essential energy.

In my mind's eye I see a classic image of a wing-footed sprite, neither male nor female, moving so fast that s/he appears and disappears, effortlessly leaping from one place to another and with complete fluidity. Each time s/he is dressed differently and holding different things out for me to see. First s/he holds up the Caduceus, then a golden globe, then two balls of shimmering silver light that s/he spins delightfully in opposite directions, one on top of the other, and then on the tip of her finger!

Then s/he is holding up her finger to her lips in the universal gesture of silence and beckoning me to enter a ball of energy that is expanding now before me. I step inside and we float together in the ethereal energy of Light.

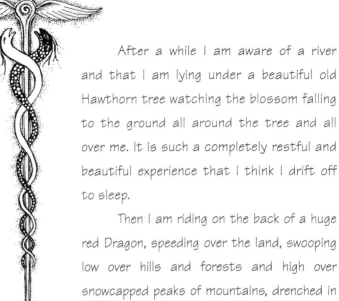

After a while I am aware of a river and that I am lying under a beautiful old Hawthorn tree watching the blossom falling to the ground all around the tree and all over me. It is such a completely restful and beautiful experience that I think I drift off to sleep.

Then I am riding on the back of a huge red Dragon, speeding over the land, swooping low over hills and forests and high over snowcapped peaks of mountains, drenched in a vivid red of sunset. I am both the rider on the back of the Dragon and the observer sitting on the mountain top, watching the Dragon fly off over the mountains into the sunset.

I welcome this mercurial mutability as part of myself. I celebrate my ability to travel the endless possibilities of the imagination, catching the inner journeys and daydreams that connect my conscious and unconscious minds together.

I welcome Hermes Mercurius as part of myself and instantly I have a vision of her/m as she steps inside my body. I see us both as Light and energy, see us both merging into One, so that now I am Hermes Mercurius and Hermes Mercurius is me. I

hold my Caduceus high, celebrating how this makes me feel. I am laughing, full of joy and a little light-headed, ethereal, as if I am made of Light. I feel I am no longer confined to my body as my conscious mind is fused with my subconscious and I become a new energy, united and whole, poised and ready to test my abilities from this new place within myself.

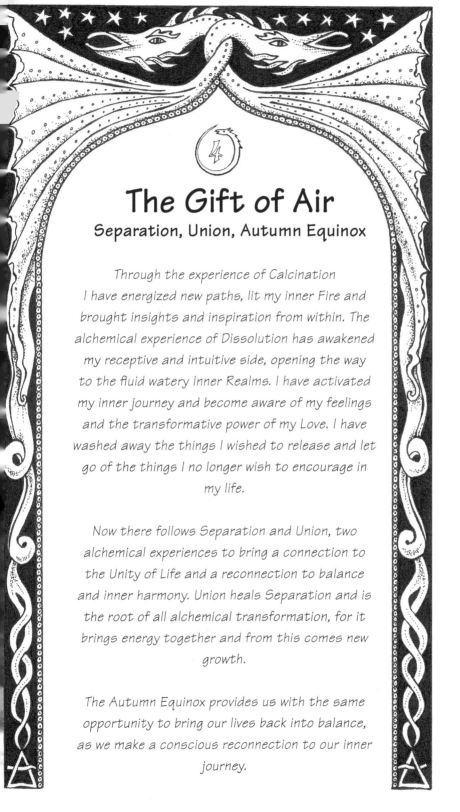

The Gift of Air
Separation, Union, Autumn Equinox

*Through the experience of Calcination
I have energized new paths, lit my inner Fire and
brought insights and inspiration from within. The
alchemical experience of Dissolution has awakened
my receptive and intuitive side, opening the way
to the fluid watery Inner Realms. I have activated
my inner journey and become aware of my feelings
and the transformative power of my Love. I have
washed away the things I wished to release and let
go of the things I no longer wish to encourage in
my life.*

*Now there follows Separation and Union, two
alchemical experiences to bring a connection to
the Unity of Life and a reconnection to balance
and inner harmony. Union heals Separation and is
the root of all alchemical transformation, for it
brings energy together and from this comes new
growth.*

*The Autumn Equinox provides us with the same
opportunity to bring our lives back into balance,
as we make a conscious reconnection to our inner
journey.*

The Alchemical Experience of Separation

Separation is the chemical process that relates to the separation of a substance into its component parts. Separation is also the alchemical metaphor for filtering and examining what has been released in the Dissolution experience. The separated parts are revealed and named so that they can be brought back together into Unity.

The alchemical experience of Separation opens the door to understanding where I become disconnected from Unity. I ask myself, 'What separates me from following my deepest longings and highest ideals? What separates me from staying connected to my heart and my loving response? How do I become separated from acting on my intuition?'

I look for the triggers, the situations and the things I am doing that create disconnection. I look for where I feel uncomfortable or unhappy or become negative. I look for what separates me from Universal Love and my spiritual path. I have to look at myself and my life with complete honesty. I am seeking out my base metal, my alchemist's Lead, the things that weigh me down and will eventually make me ill if they are not transformed. First I have to identify them before I can transform them into my Gold.

Once I have looked for where Separation manifests in my life, then I simply apply its positive opposite, what it has become separated from, superimposing a positive perception over the negative one. The energy changes immediately, for they are both parts of the same whole, and the difficulty, the disconnection, is transformed into Unity. In this way I transform fear with trust, blame with forgiveness, feelings of lack with feelings of gratitude. I transform irritation with Love and good humour, resentment with responsibility for my own feelings. I let go of my need to control and it becomes the source of my freedom! It's beautiful how it works! This is alchemy in action and it fills me with delight!

I know that from this perspective I can no longer blame anyone else for what happens to our world. With this view, the us and them' mentality is transformed into a 'we' mentality. We are the ones who are responsible for creating the kind of world we wish to live in. We are all co-creating every moment of our future.

The Alchemical Experience of Union

The experience of Union is at the heart of alchemy. Chemically, it is the recombining of the saved elements from the processes of Separation and Dissolution to form a new substance. Alchemically, Union heals separation and creates a fertile new force.

Union opens the door to the interconnected Web of Life, to Oneness, beyond the divisions of duality and polarity and the separate dimensions of Time and Space. Union is called the Opening of the Matrix'. It is opening the door to the place of infinite possibilities at the centre, as two become One. The Vesica Piscis (see page 13) is a symbolic model of how this works.

In alchemy this is known as the 'Chymical Wedding', the joining of Sol, the Sun, the Yang principle, with Luna, the Moon, the Yin principle. It is the Union of the conscious mind with the unconscious mind, the Macrocosm with the Microcosm, Heaven with Earth, 'Above with Below', the inner world with the outer.

Now there begins a powerful and exciting part of my journey, as I explore the openings that are created through the process of Union. I play with opposites and unlock the Unity at their heart, joining receptivity with action, spontaneity with planning, receiving with giving. I no longer experience these as polarities but as integrated parts of the same thing. I no longer see them as static but fluid, one flowing into the other.

I look at the old patterns of duality that have ruled my life. I know that I have been controlled and limited by these man-made divisions, by the 'us and them' mentality that has brought separation, conflict and competition into all our lives. I seek freedom from the limitations and restrictions of polarity by uniting their separated parts, so that I live my life from a place of wholeness and balance.

I become this integrated Unity. It is a powerful

transformative energy. It is inside me. I see all the classic paradoxes as part of one united whole. Good and evil, Heaven and Hell, creation and destruction, Life and death are all interconnected, rejuvenating parts of the same energy, open-ended, each a part of the other, like the Yin Yang symbol, a united energy, powerful, vibrant, full of movement and potential.

I do not seek to tame these opposites. I do not seek a bland emptiness but a vibrant equilibrium, alive with powerful forces, balanced and whole, full of potential for rejuvenation, continuance and transmutation. I do not insist on certainty, a 'proved as fact' hypothesis, or on being right, for this just becomes static, another closed door. Union is a fluid state, full of the creative energy of the fertile Life Force.

I use the visual stimulus of the Vesica Piscis symbol as my inspiration. I learn to surrender to the moment, to the opening that is created out of Union. This is the place where transformation happens, the 'place in between' and the 'place on the edge', where new energy is created.

I learn how to jump into the opening, how to merge and melt, to go with the flow, go beyond my need to control it. I learn how to trust in chaos, rest in fluidity, to simply 'be' and to wait and see what is revealed. I am learning how to trust in the process and how to ride on the swinging pendulum between the extremes of opposites until I discover the still place at the centre, the opening of the Matrix. Then I jump through the opening into a new understanding and new levels of awareness are revealed.

The Alchemy of Air

Air is the breath of Life, the connecting force, uniting all the people on the Earth and all the airbreathing creatures. We in turn are connected to all the trees and all the plants that convert the carbon dioxide we breathe out into the oxygen-rich mixture we need to breathe in. Through Air we are joined as one family, one world. Air brings Unity.

Air is also sound and all sound is vibration. Sound has energy and power. The power of the word was taken very seriously by the ancient cultures. In most of the world's religions, creation begins with the spoken word. Every sound creates a vibration that affects the vibrating universe, and every vibration goes out and returns through the intricate interconnected Web of Life, creating change in so many unseen and undreamed of ways.

In alchemy and in the Celtic system, Air is the element of communication and the mind, and this is reflected in the essential energy of Hermes Mercurius, who brings messages to Earth from the other worlds; in Sylphs, whose voices may be heard on the breeze; and in Angels and Spirit Guides, who send us messages from the Spirit Realms.

Sound and words have always been used to make connection to the unseen forces. Shamanic healers use sound, drumming, mantras, chanting and words of power to transmute illnesses and toxins and restore harmony. I believe we are all able to reverse pollution on the Earth and regenerate cancerous cells within us. It is already being done and if some people can do it then we are all capable of doing it. We just have to unlock the ability lying dormant within us. Belief and absolute trust open the doors to this, while disbelief and doubt close them off. I am willing to keep an open mind.

To connect to the element of Air I need only to focus on my breath. I mostly breathe unconsciously, but I can also choose to breathe consciously, drawing the goodness of the Air deep inside myself, picturing the oxygen enriching every cell in my body. Eastern philosophers, mystics and healers believe that the body's vital energy is carried by Air. In India this is called Prana and in China and Japan, Chi or Ki.

With my conscious breath I breathe in what I wish to energize. I use the power of sound and words to call towards me whatever I wish to activate, visualizing the energy I am creating as it makes the connections and links that give it Life.

I release what I no longer need on the out-breath, to join with the rest of the Air around me. I use the out-breath to send energy, sounds and words out and I picture their energy-making connection in the same moment that I send it. Air is not linear but a continuous circling motion. In this way everything I send out also comes back to me.

I also sing and tone notes to create a connection and to send healing. To 'tone' is to let out a note through any of the vowel sounds and hold it throughout each out-breath. This creates a harmonic resonance that is a powerful healer, bringing harmony and reconnection to the whole.

To clear a space of any disharmony or unhelpful vibration, I use a variety of bells and chimes, from large deep bells that break up a stagnant atmosphere to smaller bells that bring a refined purity to a space. I follow my intuition, extending my awareness to 'feel' the transformation the sound is creating.

The same technique can be applied to healing the body. Chimes, bells and the voice can be used to break up disharmony and to realign the body into harmonic Unity.

As well as using the physical qualities of sound, I also use the power of my thoughts to visualize Unity and harmony restored. Our thoughts are able to travel beyond the limitations of our bodies and beyond Time and Space. I can 'pick up' other people's thoughts and by the same token they can 'receive' mine. I know that I am sending out messages all the time, with every thought I have. These thoughts, and the words I am saying, are reflections of my inner feelings and the way I perceive Life.

Meditation helps me see more clearly the messages I am sending to myself and to others. I am able to hear the the chatter in my mind and reframe the thoughts by creating positive affirmations that will encourage and attract beneficial change and Unity.

The Alchemy of the Autumn Equinox

The Autumn Equinox is between September 20th and 23rd in the Northern Hemisphere and March 20th and 23rd in the Southern Hemisphere. It is the balance point when day and night are equal in length. The Earth is also balanced between the two extremes of the year: the Midsummer Solstice, the longest day, and the Midwinter Solstice, the longest night (see chart on page 27). At this point the Earth is poised before it moves into the Yin cycle and the darkest time of the year.

The Autumn Equinox is a point of Union and balance between the Light and the Dark, between Fire and Water, between the Yang and the Yin. We have all been encouraged to become disconnected from our Yin, the intuitive, 'feeling' parts of ourselves, when in reality both our Yin and Yang aspects create the whole self and, if they are not blocked, flow in a continuous holistic motion of Unity and equilibrium. The alchemy of this is seen when we join up the dots in the Yin Yang symbol to reveal the continuously flowing symbol of Infinity (see page 10).

The Autumn Equinox reminds me to balance all parts of myself, the active and the passive, the known and the unknown, the outer journey and the inner journey, the seen and the unseen, the logical and the intuitive, the conscious and the unconscious. From this place of Unity new doors open, new directions and new possibilities are revealed.

This is traditionally a time for getting in touch with gratitude and thanksgiving. It is the time of abundance on the Earth, as the harvest is gathered in, and is a moment to give thanks for all the food we eat and for all the Earth's resources that we use.

There is alchemy in this, for through my gratitude and appreciation, I give something back, and my relationship to the Earth is transformed because of it. I have created an energetic connection between my heart, my feelings and the Earth. This Unity creates a vibration of Love and respect. The ancient people understood how important this was and would not take anything without first offering thanks or an exchange of some kind. Giving and receiving are the same. When they are united as One, the door to the flow of increase and abundance is open.

At this time of the Earth's harvest, I look at my own personal harvest — what has come to fruition in my personal life, what I have learned from my experiences. I am aware that the Earth's energy is about to change and I follow Nature's lead, gradually closing down the outer world and opening up to the inner world, preparing for rest, regeneration and reconnection to my roots.

The Sun has ripened the fruit on the outside and inside lie the seeds from which next year's harvest will grow. As I look at my personal harvest, I also look for the seeds that lie hidden within it, the seeds that I will nurture in the dark of the winter. It is time to gather my seeds, my resources, to look within, to seek wisdom in the dark of the year, to find renewal in rest and to explore hidden parts of myself.

I am learning to listen to my inner voice, to value and develop my inner senses, to trust my intuition, to follow my heart, to find balance and wholeness in myself, in my life and in the world. True spirituality is growing within me. I am becoming more caring and nurturing, more compassionate and loving, more aware of my feelings and how these are connected to the feelings of others.

September 5th
The Elementals

Today I am meeting up with some close friends to share sacred space together. We are five women and we fondly call ourselves the 'Elementals'. We meet regularly, taking time out from our busy lives to share our spiritual connections. We all have our own unique understanding of spirituality and this adds to our diversity and our ability to accept each person's unique journey.

We meet in our homes to celebrate each of the eight Celtic festivals, which fall once every six weeks, but we also meet once in between these times for inner journeying, healing and creative energy work. We always create ceremony together, share healing and alchemy and connect to our spiritual journey. We sometimes have special days out to sacred and powerful places in our local landscape, or we walk in the woods. We plan positive actions to bring change into the world and support each other in planning and facilitating workshops. We always bring food and drink to share and we are always lifted and heartened by our time together.

We reclaim the old meaning of the word 'conspiracy', which means 'breathing together', and we use our breath and our words for creative acts of alchemy and healing.

Tonight we are meeting to do some energy work. We sit in a circle and create sacred space by energizing each of the Five Elements through our breath and the power of sound. We all hum and tone notes, words and sounds, blending them all together as we focus on the transformative and healing qualities of each of the Five Elements.

When this is done we take it in turns to share what feels important to us at this point in time and what we want to do today. Often we are not clear about what we will do until it grows out of this 'check-in'.

Tonight we decide to work with the transformative alchemy of Air and begin by singing chants together, opening up our heart connection to each other and to our deepest feelings, opening up our lungs and throat, letting our creative harmonies flow. Our breath and our songs are strong and expansive, uniting us in a beautiful swirling flow of sound and energy.

We then agree to consciously use our out-breath to lovingly release whatever we wish to let go of, to picture the old unwanted energy dispersing into the wind, into tiny specks floating off to join the cosmos. We whisper and sing their release, all whispering our words and singing at the same time. We sing for ourselves and we sing for the Earth and all our words and notes blend together to create a remarkable harmonious whole.

Then we breathe in what we wish to draw towards ourselves and sing our connection to what we wish to energize. We echo each other's words until we are circulating all the words and sounds together, energizing their power for ourselves, for each other and for the world.

After this we sit in silence, in stillness and contemplation.

I contemplate our freedom and choice to change our thoughts and perceptions by changing the words and the phrases that we use. We can create our own mantras, simple phrases that help us to generate a new perception or new way of thinking.

We can breathe Life into any new direction we choose.

We decide to activate some new positive words for ourselves, words that will help us to establish new thought patterns and transform ways of thinking that we want to change.

We all sing out our new words or phrases, overlapping each other's words in a glorious celebration of positivity.

We are loud and exuberant and end on a Cone of Power, each toning long single notes and merging them together, harmonizing all our notes into one united vibration. Through this Cone of Power we visualize all our new words and phrases inside ourselves and send them off into Spirit. Our journey of transformation has begun!

After our meeting I am more aware of the words that hold energy for me. I notice the words I use frequently and the vibration that comes with them. I like it when I use the words 'wonderful', 'beautiful', 'perfect' and 'gorgeous'. I notice the words and phrases I use when I am distressed, angry and unloving, and I am gradually able to use these negative words as trigger points. They are a reminder to me to stop and change what I am saying and sending out. When I replace the negative words with positive phrases, this creates an alchemical shift in the energy I am creating.

Communication goes both ways and what I am sending out to the world I am also sending to myself, thus affecting my own health and well-being as well as the health and wellbeing of others. My awareness of this alchemy is growing and I take this with me on my inner journey.

September 16th

Autumn Equinox Harvest

The forest floors are absolutely full of acorns this year. I have never seen such abundance! They are everywhere, in their thousands! They are so beautiful and colourful – pinks and greens, oranges and browns. Some are sprouting already where they lie. I cannot stop myself from picking them up. Each one is perfect and unique and before long my pockets are full of acorns. And now I have them, I can't put them down again! I am aware that they cannot grow here in the woods; there is no more room. I feel connected to their brave new energy, to the little shoot that will become the root which will delve deep into the Earth and, if given the chance, grow into a mighty Oak tree. I am struck by the thought that these beautiful acorns could still be living as trees in 400 years' time and that just 50 of these little acorns could become a small wood. I easily have half that amount in my pocket!

So I take them home and leave them outside in the wind and the rain for a while, enjoying the look of them lying in a broken clay pot on its side by my door. On the New Moon I plant them in damp compost, several in each plant pot. I am filled with the thought that from little acorns, mighty Oaks will grow, and from small actions, mighty changes will grow. Next autumn I'll pot them up for another year before eventually finding places to plant them out. I feel a little *daunted by this, as I have so many, but I trust that I will find places for them when the time comes.*

Right now I am filled with the pleasure that the acorns have brought me, the look and feel of them as I was collecting them in the woods and the enjoyment I have had planting them, knowing that they have a good chance of becoming trees.

I return in my thoughts to the Kings Oak on the Glastonbury festival site and I remember its beauty and picture how it must look now in its autumn colours. I remember my vision of the balanced wholeness of the tree, an equal amount of roots branching out into the dark of the earth to balance the visible branches stretching outwards to the sunlight and the moonlight. I imagine myself joining again with the energy of the Kings Oak and remember the message to follow what truly inspires me. I know that this is influencing my journey now. I write 'I follow what truly inspires me' on a piece of card and decorate it with a pattern of Oak leaves, so that I see it often and remember.

Alchemical Symbols of Union and Transformation

Imagery is an essential part of Air alchemy. Through the use of images and symbols I am able to go beyond the limitations of words and communicate on different levels.

Using symbols is an act of Union. We unite the symbol with the conscious mind and out of this grows a new understanding. Our understanding of a symbol lies in the 'in-between' place, neither in the conscious nor the unconscious. Symbols and imagery open the door to a fluidity and freedom within the mind.

There are many symbols of Union and transformation in alchemy and because alchemy is not a fixed doctrine, any symbol from any system can be used in whatever way feels right at the time. We are also free to create our own symbols with whatever has meaning for us.

I use symbols as a focus for meditation, holding them in my mind's eye with the same relaxed focused attention that I give my breath, letting layers of understanding circulate and new meanings surface from within.

I also use symbols for healing, sending them to myself when I need their energy and visualizing each symbol uniting with wherever I send it, arriving at the same moment that I send it.

I activate the energy of symbols as I draw or paint them, which helps me to internalize my understanding of them. I create them on the ground in the woods, using twigs, berries, nuts and seeds, or on the beach using stones and shells. I decorate a cake or a pie with their patterns! I dance and walk them as pathways of energy on the land, revelling in their simplicity and their fluidity.

The Infinity Symbol

The Infinity symbol is a never-ending dance of flow and continuous cycles, without beginning or end. It crosses the boundaries of right and left-brain activity when I follow its path. It is found in science and mathematics as well as alchemy and esoteric systems.

I use it to bring joining, harmony and balance and to open my connection to the eternal flowing Unity of the interconnected Web of Life.

The Ouroboros and the Power of the Circle

The Ouroboros is the Greek name for the Hermetic serpent of alchemy, the snake or serpent that swallows its own tail. It is sometimes called the World Serpent and sometimes the sea serpent Oceanus, which encircles the Earth. It is also known as the Worm and is linked to Earth energy, the Earth Dragon and the Dragon Paths or serpent force that links ancient sites and places of power. It represents the continuous cycles of Life, the fundamental Life Force, our most primitive responses and needs, and what is hidden in the Dark.

The Ouroboros is also a symbol of the cyclic nature of Eternity. The journey is never completed. With every end there is always a new beginning. Everything is always in a process of transformation and change. So the Ouroboros represents all cyclic alternations beyond polarity: Light as part of Dark, Dark as part of Light; birth as part of death, death as part of birth; summer as part of winter, winter as part of summer; Love as part of hate, hate as part of Love. It represents the alchemy of the Union of Matter with Spirit, Spirit with Matter, always joined together in one continuous circuit. This is the central Unity and power of the Circle, healing, uniting and never-ending.

The Equilateral Triangle

The equilateral triangle represents the Trinity, a symbol of Unity that is found in all religions and all cultures. In alchemy it represents the balanced Unity of mind, body and Spirit and in the old alchemical texts it represented the joining of the chemicals Salt, Sulphur and Mercury. Each of the Four Elements of Life is represented as an equilateral triangle: Fire, Air, Earth and Water.

The triangle represents equality, stability and fluidity. Its points can be joined to create an outer circle, and the

FIRE   AIR   EARTH   WATER

mid-points between the two united energies can be joined to create an inner circle, creating wholeness, cyclic movement and Unity.

The Six-Pointed Star

In alchemy the sixpointed star is Quintessence. All of the alchemical symbols of Earth, Air, Fire and Water are joined together to become One, the Fifth Element, Spirit or Ether, the Essence of all things, Cosmic Unification, Perfection.

The six-pointed star also has the power of two triangles – twice the Trinity. It represents the alchemist's maxim 'As Above So Below', 'As Within, So Without' and the conscious joining of the Above with the Below, Spirit with Matter.

When all the six-pointed star's outer points are joined together it becomes the hexagram. This is found in Nature in the honeycomb, home of bees, who show us the uniting power of community and working together to support the whole.

October 4th

Planting the Alchemy of Love

Today I am planting bulbs in large pots to put outside next to my doors. With my hands in the dark wet compost I am reminded of the growth that will continue beneath the Earth and will resurface in the spring. Each bulb represents something I would like to see grow and with each bulb I plant I say a pledge or make a connection. I also plant bulbs for my family and my sacred kin, especially the young children that I have special friendships with. I plant a special pot for Rowan, my friend's baby, whose birth it was my great honour and delight to be present at. I am still filled with the powerful 'presence' which she brought with her as she made her great journey into Life. I plant each bulb with Love, which I send to the person I plant it for. I mix the different varieties up so that each pot will be a surprise in the spring.

As I plant the bulbs I focus on the power of Universal Love as a force for change in the world. Love restores Unity. It is a great bridge-builder and I harness the power of its Unity as a focus for our similarities as humans. Love heals divisions and has the power to heal the hurts of generations and the hurts of nations. It is an energy that crosses the great divides, such as the great division of Past, Present and Future. It fuses them all together in this one moment, the only moment we truly have, which is NOW!

Universal Love is available to us all, an infinite resource we all have, whatever our age, gender, colour, nationality or creed. We can all feel it and experience the change it creates. There is not one of us who is not able to access Love. If each one of us makes the choice to find it in ourselves and use it as often as we can, and if enough people choose to do this, then the world will change.

The cyclic nature of all Life in the natural world suggests that communication is also cyclic. When we communicate we create an energy link that returns the energy to the sender. Giving is linked to receiving, and always the energy that is sent out, be it Life-enhancing or destructive, will return. I feel this in a very immediate way when I send the energy of Universal Love. I feel filled up inside with the same thing that I am sending. For Love just keeps on multiplying and it transforms anything it touches into itself. It is my alchemist's Gold, my Philosopher's Stone and my Elixir of Life. The more Love I give, the more Love is released into world and the more comes back to me.

October 6th
Love, Unity and Healing

I light candles with the Love Fire of the Peace Flame and sit in peaceful contemplation of Love, Unity and healing. I send 'energy messages' out into the world, fusing Love, Unity and healing into One. I do this by connecting to this united energy within myself at the same time as sending it out to where it is needed. I believe my ability to do this is improving the more I do it. Absent healing is as powerful as the laying on of hands and when I send out the healing energy I visualize the healing, the sending and the receiving as One, united in the same moment. I know that my clarity and *inner certainty are crucial here, for doubt will block the flow.*

I myself have received absent healing from others, often with dramatic effects, and I have also had confirmation back from others that the healing I have sent has made a difference. This is my personal proof of its effectiveness. I don't need it to be proved scientifically. I don't need it to be logical. I have the truth of my own experience.

Over the last 20 years there have been many meditation, interfaith, prayer and healing link-ups sending Universal Love and healing to people and areas of conflict and disaster and visualizing world Peace and healing for the Earth. These global co-operation events raise consciousness and support Peace and Unity worldwide. This in turn unites the people of the world who believe in their ability to create change in this way. (See Contacts, pages 275–6.)

Of course the effectiveness of these meditation, prayer and healing link-ups cannot be measured, but if I can feel the effect of one person sending me Love and healing, I believe that great healing is being brought into the world by the united power of many.

October 12th

Spirit of Transformation

I am aware of the way the Earth has let go of her great growth cycle now. There has been such a lot of rain and the element of water has been very present, washing clean the Earth and revitalizing the air. Everything is refreshed by it. The last of the garden apples and pears are falling to the ground and now the winds come and lash at the trees. I see the changes, hear the changes and feel the changes that are coming as one cycle ends and with it comes the potential for new beginnings.

Today I go out walking in the woods. It is a wild, changeable day full of shifting clouds and alternating weather. The leaves are clattering down through the branches of the trees and brilliant shafts of sunlight suddenly burst through the woods. I am aware of the leaves falling to join layer upon layer of other leaves that have fallen in other years. Each tree stands in the midst of its own shedding leaves, surrounded by a perfect circle of orange on the dark floor of the woods.

At this time of year the trees teach me about letting go and about the cyclic nature of Life. All of Life is transition, transformation and change. The leaves fall, become compost and provide nutrition for the tree's roots and seeds. Nothing in nature is linear; everything connects back up to itself in cycles. With a tree, the shedding of the year's growth ensures its fertility and future growth. This awareness helps me in how I live my life. I am full of wonder at the transition and movement of Life's cycles. There are no endings; everything is in the process of change, creating equilibrium and Union with itself.

Today I have a real sense of my journey through life, a wonderful journey of discovery and interconnected experiences which return their wisdom to me. I feel I am gradually becoming more conscious of this multi-dimensional world, better able to enter the infinite interconnected Web of possibilities, the Infinite Life of the Matrix. I unite with this timeless place through my imagination, inner journeying and meditation, and through this Union I discover more about who I am. It is all a matter of perception – a shift in perception and I have opened another door to another reality. I am aware that when I imagine it, I also experience it. This is food for thought that I take with me into the Dark of the year.

I am drawn towards an old grandmother Chestnut tree and go and sit with her, leaning my back against her trunk. I slow my breathing down and settle my energy in with the tree, letting my thoughts fall away like leaves to the Earth. I slip out of Time and begin to daydream, imagining myself as a small animal curled up in the roots of the tree, sleeping and drifting into hibernation for the winter. I feel the comfort and warmth of the tree holding me. We breathe together in the dark safe Earth.

I become aware of a string of thoughts I am having about making food with conscious awareness of the energy that is transferred into it during the preparation and cooking process. It is a good thought, perhaps sparked by my desire to gather chestnuts. I send my Love and thanks to grandmother Chestnut tree and gather many chestnuts to take home with me.

I make a chestnut roast with them, remembering to be aware of the energy I am putting into the food as I prepare and cook it. I am filled with gratitude for the Earth, for my family, for my friends, for my life, so the nut roast is very potent food indeed, full of the Spirit of the woods, the grandmother Chestnut, my deep Love and gratitude and feelings of Oneness with all Life. This alchemy fills me with delight, as it is rooted in the power and simplicity of everyday life. A shift in perception and I have opened another door to another reality.

October 22nd

Compost

I wake early this morning and look out of the window. The compost bins are steaming eerily in the golden dawn light, reminding me again about compost. So this morning I ask myself, 'What is it that I wish to compost this year? What shall I shed, like leaves from my tree? What shall I let go of so that it can be transformed in the Dark of the winter months into my inner journey? What new seeds, new possibilities could grow from this?'

I don't have any immediate answers, but I am thinking about it all day on and off. By the evening I am ready to tune into sacred space. This will help me focus on any answers that come to the surface. I ask my family not to disturb me for an hour, switch off my phone and prepare for an inner journey.

I begin by gathering a few things together – a warm blanket to wrap around myself and something to represent each of the Five Elements. I send Love and gratitude to a bowl of spring water to honour the Spirit of Water. For Fire I light a new candle, saying, 'For release and balance.' To represent Earth I find a few flowers from the garden, precious now that the autumn is ending, also the stone egg I found at the spring. These will anchor my understanding and insights. To represent Air I have a feather I found in the woods and a bamboo whistle.

I switch off the light and settle myself very comfortably with plenty of cushions, legs crossed, the blanket wrapped around me. I begin by taking lots of slow, deep breaths and feel that I am wrapping a nurturing energy all around myself. Even if I do nothing more, this feels so good – a welcome shutdown.

I take up the bamboo whistle and begin to play. I am not a whistle player, but I love to put notes together. I play long low notes, releasing my breath gently into the whistle and slipping into a meditative state. I don't play for long, but it's enough to create a change in mood and atmosphere. I keep my mind focused on the candle flame and my intention: 'For release and balance.'

I picture each of the Five Elements forming a circle around me and connecting to me on the inside and the outside at the same time. I feel the energy of connection and Union flow into me and out of me in a continuous Infinite Flow of energy and Light, flowing all around me, spreading outwards and inwards at the same time, connecting me to the timeless Matrix.

I keep focused on my breath, consciously aware of each breath in and each breath out. I take full breaths, my breathing slows and eventually I find myself in an effortless rhythmic place, centred and aligned, rather detached from my thoughts and my body, very still and very empty.

I picture my roots going down into the Earth below me, below the house, rooting me here and connecting me to a deep-rooted place inside me at the same time. I have a sense of being 'all joined up', connected to the deep knowing that is always there within me, complete, whole, healthy, loving, the 'Above and Below' in perfect balance. I feel part of the Unity of Life, and also unique and individual. I let these feelings and understandings flow through me, taking them inside on my in-breath and sending them out into the world on my out-breath, mixing them all up as I float into a deeply connected ocean.

I have been drifting for some time when I remember that I had a quest, a question that I wanted to ask myself. What have I learned from this year's experiences? What of my spring seeds? What has grown well and what hasn't? I cast my mind back to the things I did during the spring, the summer and the autumn, gathering them towards myself with gratitude.

I visualize them as leaves on my tree, then visualize myself as the tree. I see myself in a clearing with Birch trees all around me. But I am a Chestnut tree, with the Sun shining brightly on my golden leaves. Patterns of light and shadow are everywhere and everything is moving in a gentle breeze and vibrant with Life and energy.

I enjoy this vision, and stay connected to it for some time, watching birds come and go, feeling peaceful and at One with everything around me. Then I remember my leaves and let go of all my achievements, my understandings and insights, my hurts, my uncertainties, my needs, my disappointments, my joys. I let everything go as my leaves fall around me, dripping leaves, falling leaves, leaves bathed in sunlight, leaves bathed in moonlight, letting go, letting go, letting go, until I feel complete, clear and remarkably filled up and empty at the same time. I see all my leaves lying all around me and send my Love into the compost they will make.

I pick up the bamboo whistle and join some notes slowly together. Long breaths of sound fill the room, gradually bringing me back into my body. My eyes fall on the stone egg and I hold it for a while, anchoring myself back into Earth. I use the stone to hold and anchor the experience, storing my journey and my understanding inside it. I drinkthe spring water, taking in its stored memory. I stare at the candle flame and enjoy the slowness of arriving back.

I write down the understanding that I gained from the journey, my awareness of the balanced place, the alchemical Union within me, the things I was able to let go of, the compost I made. My new seeds are there, unformed and waiting. Let them lie in the Dark! Their time will come!

HERMES MERCURIUS

In alchemy, the principle of Unity is symbolized by Hermes Mercurius. The Caduceus s/he carries is a symbol of our ability to heal polarity and divisions and to activate healing from the Unity within ourselves. Her art is healing-through-communication. S/he is able to communicate on many different levels across the multi-dimensional universe with complete ease and fluidity. This ability is also in me.

I am open to whatever this ancient archetype has to teach me and I meditate on where to find her energy inside myself.

It is here in my Heart chakra, in the power of Universal Love, which heals and transforms all it touches. It is here in my Third Eye chakra at the centre of my brow, the seat of my spiritual awareness and an interface between the world within and the world without.

In between these two chakras lies my Throat chakra, where I communicate with the world. This is the bridge between the truth in my heart and the truth of my spiritual awareness, which I communicate through my words and my thoughts.

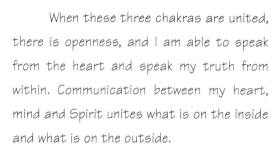

When these three chakras are united, there is openness, and I am able to speak from the heart and speak my truth from within. Communication between my heart, mind and Spirit unites what is on the inside and what is on the outside.

Hermes Mercurius inspires me to practise the art of uniting Spirit with Matter, the invisible with the visible, to create a bridge across the great divide. Their Union creates fluidity and freedom within me. Energy is set in motion and new possibilities are opened up.

Through my mind and imagination I can join with others, send Love and Harmony, picture any future, send healing and open any number of doors and energy pathways. I can merge, join, unite, commune, combine, harmonize, integrate, synchronize and create concordance. I can create links to whatever I choose and sense the harmonic resonance this creates. Out of any of the combined links I create comes new energy. I sense the place of Unity in between the two, the place of all possibilities, where a new energy has Life.

I take this seed and plant it in the Dark. I take this understanding inside myself, to strengthen it during my inner journey.

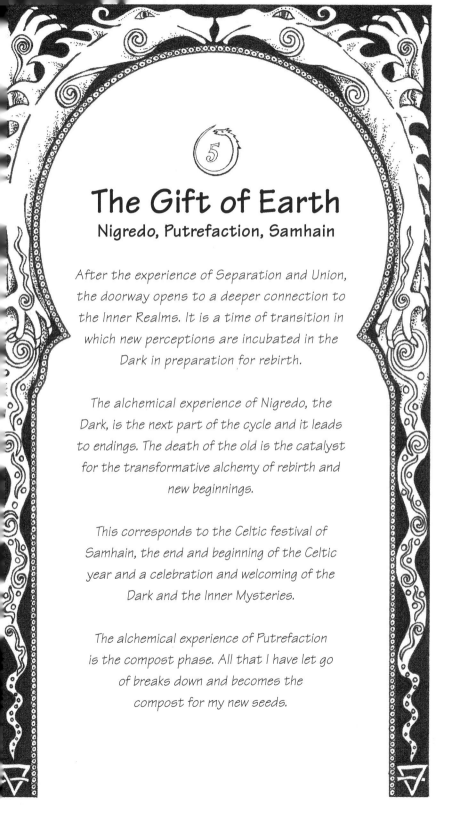

5

The Gift of Earth
Nigredo, Putrefaction, Samhain

After the experience of Separation and Union,
the doorway opens to a deeper connection to
the Inner Realms. It is a time of transition in
which new perceptions are incubated in the
Dark in preparation for rebirth.

The alchemical experience of Nigredo, the
Dark, is the next part of the cycle and it leads
to endings. The death of the old is the catalyst
for the transformative alchemy of rebirth and
new beginnings.

This corresponds to the Celtic festival of
Samhain, the end and beginning of the Celtic
year and a celebration and welcoming of the
Dark and the Inner Mysteries.

The alchemical experience of Putrefaction
is the compost phase. All that I have let go
of breaks down and becomes the
compost for my new seeds.

The Alchemical Experience of Nigredo

Chemically, the substance in the flask is broken down into its base components, becoming black decaying matter. In the symbolism of alchemy, the Sun is eclipsed and all is in darkness. Alchemically, Nigredo, the Dark, is the ending of one cycle, out of which new possibilities are revealed. It begins with a descent into the Darkness inside us to find the Lead, which is also the Gold, the alchemist's Prime Substance or Base Matter, the very essence of Life.

Darkness has been associated with fear and evil in our culture for hundreds of years, but it was not always so. To the Celts and the ancient civilizations, the Dark was celebrated as a place inside us where we touch and experience our spiritual roots and was known as the Mysteries. Nigredo is an experience of this deep connection to our spirituality.

I reclaim the Dark as the part of myself where I rest in stillness. This is where I reconnect to my inner feelings and my spirituality, a place of rejuvenation and transformation that I celebrate as a natural part of my whole self.

Through meditation, the art of being and contemplation I find stillness within. I am able to touch my deepest wisdom and find my connection to my natural goodness and inner knowing at my core. I find my connection to Spirit and the Gold that lies within.

As I come into the winter months, the dark nights and shorter days help me to slow down, return to base, rest inside myself. I remind myself to slow down my activities in the outer world and open up to my inner world.

As part of the alchemical cycle, Nigredo is also an opportunity for me to explore my emotional depths at the deepest level. I become aware of where I am disconnected from Love and where I am emotionally stuck. It is a time for Soul-searching as I face what I have repressed or neglected to deal with, my deep fears, unhappiness and resentments that may linger and tie me to the past. They are my Lead. They weigh me down and stop me from moving forward. They will eventually manifest as illness if they are not transformed. I let them come to the surface, like bubbles coming up from a muddy pool. I jump into the chaos, see my shadow side, walk on the edge of my own sanity and allow these aspects of myself to exist.

All the alchemical experiences so far can be brought into play as I face what has been buried and bring it out into the open. I activate my path forwards by finding my Sacred Fire, my connection to Spirit (Calcination). I let go of old hurts and all the things that I no longer need to hold on to, releasing them, dissolving the ties that bind me to the past. I let them go, let them go, as many times as it takes, until I really feel a sense of clarity and freedom (Dissolution). I unite my Lead with the Gold of Universal Love, I unite my negative feelings with their positive opposite and they reveal their Unity and the potential hidden at the centre (Separation and Union). I am now free to rest, to create new beginnings that will lead to further transformation and the potential to create more Gold.

I find my Gold in the darkness. It is my eternal connection to Spirit, my Essence, my heart and my Soul. Through it I am united with the Web of Life and the transformative power of Universal Love. In the darkness I find a place to rest and be still for long enough to be able to experience this valuable part of myself and to experience this inner wisdom with all of my being.

The Alchemical Experience of Putrefaction

Putrefaction is the decomposition of the substance in the alchemist's flask. It is part of the Nigredo experience. Alchemically, it is a composting process that comes from the release, the breaking down of all the separated parts and the letting go of all the stored negativity.

I shed my triumphs and achievements as well as my sadness, worries and failures. I let them all fall away – all the things that I have been hanging on to that have limited and bound me. They all fall away from me like leaves from my tree, to rest in the Earth. They become my compost as they rot and decay. As all gardeners know, good compost creates good fertile soil in which to grow healthy plants.

In letting go of the old I empty myself so that I can rest uncluttered, unhindered by baggage from the past. I lie back and enjoy the blackness as I dream new dreams and see the potential of new seeds.

My alchemist's flask is now full of good well-rotted compost, ready to receive the new seeds that will grow from the Nigredo and Putrefaction experience. They are my new paths, forming in the darkness. I let them rest in this fluid state, so that they flow through the subtle realms of Spirit. They soak up the goodness of the compost so that they become strong seeds, ready to grow when the time is right.

The Alchemy of Earth

Earth is where I find myself, my base camp. It is where I begin and where I return, where my physical body lives and transcends. Earth is held by gravity and Time. It keeps me anchored and grounded. Earth is a vessel, a container for my journey. It holds me as I explore who I am and through this the cycles of Life, Death and Regeneration. Through my actions I bring my inner world into manifestation.

The Earth is also the ground beneath my feet and I honour this connection to my Earth home, to the Spirit of

Gaia, the Earth Mother, nourisher and provider, the Fertile Force, place of creation, balance and continuous cycles of regeneration. This is where I manifest my dreams and create my reality.

I am rooted here in this present moment by my past. My roots go back in Time to all my Ancestors and to all the lives I may have had here before this one. My roots go deep into the Dark, the Inner Realms where Time runs differently. Through the element of Earth I am connected to what is hidden, the Mysteries, the formless chaos of fertility and all possibilities. Earth connects me to the Unity of Life, the Matrix, the Web of all possibilities. I create my future with every word, thought and deed, setting things in motion, creating connections and links. The Earth is part of me. I am Earth. Everything on the Earth is connected. We are all One.

Earth is the Regenerative Force. The Earth's cycles show me continuous Life. All is in motion, uniting parts of the whole, always becoming, continuously transforming. Out of the darkness, death and decay of the winter come spring, Life, new growth.

I use Earth alchemically to change energy. I bury things in the Earth that need to rest, to return to the Dark, or need to break down into compost and be re-absorbed into the Web of Life.

I bury things in salt to clear their energy, especially crystals that have absorbed negativity, have been worn a lot or have been used for healing.

I use a bowl of earth or compost to plant seeds of the future, seeds of hope, seeds of myself. I use the earth from my garden and also soil that I have collected from special places that have significance for me.

I plant trees, bulbs, seeds and other plants at the same time as visualizing what I wish to grow, such as an idea, an intention, a vision, a new venture or something I wish to draw into my life.

I also 'plant' stones and crystals in the ground in which energy, intentions, hopes or new directions have been stored.

When I am creating ceremony and sacred space, I use soil, compost, sand, salt, stones and crystals, as well as plants, flowers and trees to create a connection to the energy of Earth.

Earth brings structure and stability. What stabilizing structures do I choose to give myself? What unnecessary structures imposed upon me by society, religion and upbringing do I choose to free myself from?

Earth is nurturing. I learn how to nurture myself by encouraging the things that make me happy, that bring me deep inner contentment, that make me feel whole and well.

Earth brings regeneration and rejuvenation out of rest. How will I use my time of rest this year?

Earth anchors roots. How will I root my ideas in practical sustainable solutions that help my Spirit to grow?

I unite the stabilizing, grounding qualities of Earth with the way I live my life, use my time and the Earth's resources.

This helps me to develop a lifestyle that supports the Earth and the people of the Earth in sustainable and Lifeenhancing ways, through all my actions, every product that I buy and the way that I run my home.

The Alchemy of Samhain

In the Northern Hemisphere, Samhain is at the end of October/beginning of November. In the Southern Hemisphere, it is at the end of April/beginning of May (see chart on page 27). Samhain is the Celtic festival that celebrates the death of the old year and the potential for transformation that this opens up. The festival of Samhain has the same energy as the Nigredo and Putrefaction experience of alchemy. Samhain also celebrates the stillness in the Dark before the start of the new cycle and honours the in-between place, the formless and forming energy on the edge of Time.

Samhain is the beginning of the deepest, darkest part of the year, the beginning of winter, a transition point when the energy changes and everything returns to the Earth. It is one of the most powerful times in the Earth's cycle, the ending of one cycle and the beginning of another, a time for reconnection to the inner Mysteries.

In the Celtic tradition Samhain is recognized as a time when the veil between the worlds is thin and, similar to Beltain, we are able to slip through into other dimensions, the places that lie 'between the worlds'. To the Celts this was known as the Otherworld. Here we are able to communicate with the world of Spirits, our Ancestors and Descendants, Spirit Guides, Guardians and Angels, who will help us if we ask them, and sometimes even if we don't.

Here is an opportunity for me to challenge my assumptions about the world I think I know, to change my perspective, to look inside myself, to reflect, to find the openings, the doorways to fresh new insights, to the previously unseen. It is an opportunity to enter into the Dark, the Mysteries, and to dream a new dream.

I let my old self die so that I can rebirth the new. I allow myself to disintegrate so that my thoughts and ideas can reform. I dig for the Gold and look for what can be transformed.

Reclaiming the Dark

I welcome the Dark as part of my life. Each and every day, darkness brings me the night, which gives me the welcome opportunity to stop and rest, to shut down my busy mind, to assimilate and digest my day. Through dreams I am able to open a valuable interface with my transcendental self.

The daily cycle of Light and Dark is also mirrored in the Earth's yearly cycle. Winter also offers us opportunities for rest and renewal, inner reflection, digestion of the year's events and experiences.

During the winter months I am learning to develop stillness and 'the art of being'. This is an inner stillness that I reach from staring into space, just being myself without stimulation, learning how to do nothing. I don't find it easy. I want to measure my time by what I have done or achieved. But gradually I am letting go of this and am learning to value inner Peace, the stillness within. I am also learning to value daydreaming as a way of opening to the world within. Daydreaming, entering the unformed, unpredictable world of my imagination, brings me into greater balance with myself. I also find that doing art and craftwork helps to rest my mind. This kind of activity helps me to slip out of Time and into the realms of my imagination, the Inner Realms I find within myself.

The Celts called this inner world 'the Otherworld', 'the Dark' or 'between the worlds'. Ancient cultures all over the world have words and descriptions for it. It is everything outside our conscious reality, including the world of Angels, Spirit Guides, Daemons, Guardians, the Faerie Realms, the Spirit Realms, the world of Sidhe (pronounced 'She'), the realms of the Dead and the Ancestors. To the Celts, the Otherworld lay all around them and also inside them. To the alchemist and the Celtic Pagan mind, there is no separation between Spirit and Matter, it is all One. Spirit is integrated into Life, Life is reflected into Spirit.

Christianity polarized the Celtic Otherworld into Heaven, a place in the sky we must all aspire to, a place of Angels and Light, and Hell, a place to fear, a dark subterranean prison, a place of eternal pain and torture. The Christian Heaven and Hell could only be reached after death and this successfully changed the Otherworld of our Celtic Pagan roots from being an accessible part of ourselves and our everyday lives and removed it to 'the afterlife'. To the Celtic Pagans, however, there was no 'afterlife'. They saw death as a transformation, a part of the never-ending circulating energy of Life.

During the Middle Ages the Church redefined the Mysteries and so the transformative power of the Dark became distorted. The Otherworld, the Spirit Realms, the regenerative Dark, became Hell, a place of evil. Hel was previously a uterine shrine, a cave of rebirth, a place of initiation into the Mysteries. Hellenes was a Norse Queen of the Underworld, a Dark Goddess, Crone and Wise Woman who was honoured throughout the ancient world and provided an anchor for understanding the formless, timeless Inner Realms.

Celtic Dark Goddesses include Rhea-Kronia, Old Mother Time, who devoured Time itself; Rhiannon, also the Mother of Time, who devoured her own children; Cerridwen, who kept the Cauldron of Rebirth and Regeneration, and was known as the Grandmother of Memory and the Keeper of the Ancestral Gateway; Scotia, Satha, Scythia, Cailleach, the Black Mother of the Northlands; and the Old Hag or Veiled One (hag meaning 'holy woman'). Other Dark Goddesses included Kali or Kali Ma, destroying Goddess of the Hindus; Hecate, the Greek Goddess of magic, omens and prophecy, also known as Persephone, who ruled the Underworld in ancient myth and was later replaced by the male God Pluto; and Saturn, known as Old Father Time.

The myths and legends behind these archetypes, Gods and Goddesses describe the ancient view of the Otherworld and Life. The same stories are found in different cultures all over the Earth and in the collective unconscious. They are a common thread and hold clues to the natural healing power of regeneration in the Dark.

I experience the Inner Realms as a place inside myself which becomes whatever I imagine it to be. I am connected to it through my imagination, and by expanding my awareness through meditation and inner journeying (see Appendix, page 269), I keep an open mind and find ways to open the door and peep inside.

Modern physics acknowledges this inner world as the realm of sub-atomic particles that change the moment we give them any attention. They are a mirror of our subconscious thoughts, impermanent, fleeting, irrational and interconnected. Recent string theory suggests there are parallel realities, shadowy, unformed, there one moment, gone the next, worlds within worlds within worlds. This supports the ancients' view that the Otherworld is within us, that it is to each of us whatever we think it is, that we all create our own destinies in each and every fluid moment.

My Otherworld lies within me as well as all around me. It lies just outside what I experience with my five senses of sight,

smell, touch, hearing and taste, and offers an experience of my sixth sense. It is reached through the imagination, which creates links and pathways that open into this elusive world which lies on the borders between thought and Time. It is a place where Time runs differently, bringing shifts in perception and insights beyond words.

The Otherworld is a mirror, reflecting whatever perspective I bring to it, a place of mystery. It has no location other than in my mind, so there is nothing further to do than jump in and experience this creative place within myself, balanced on the edge, between the worlds.

November 7th

A Shift in Focus

Outside the days are short and often dark. The land is wet and most of the old leaves and fruit have fallen and are rotting back into the Earth. I know that the Earth is preparing for rebirth, but slowly, there's no hurry, there's time to rest a while before the busy growth cycle begins again. I feel that I too have time to rest and I shift my focus from outer achievements to the world within. I look back and I remember.

At this time I prepare my inner soil so that I create the best possible conditions for the seeds of my future growth. This means clearing out the weeds, clearing out the old beliefs, old patterns and old fears. I no longer want them!

I dig them up and visualize them piled into a hot steamy compost heap. I throw them all on – all the beliefs I have carried for so long that say I am not good enough, not heard, not understood, not valued, all those that say I am in the wrong. I no longer need them! I laugh with the joy of it! All the old unwanted parts of myself are breaking up and breaking down and forming nutritious new soil for my new seeds! I forgive myself for all the missed opportunities of the old year, all the moments I could have handled better, the times I could have been more thoughtful, more loving, more centred. I accept my year, I accept myself as I am, right now, doing my best, in this moment. And I move on.

I also have a good clearout in my living space, throwing away or giving away anything that stops me moving forward – all the things from the past that hold me back, all the clutter I no longer need.

Afterwards I give everything that is left a good clean and then I use the Five Elements to clear and re-energize my space.

I use the transformative energy of Water and wash everything in running water to clear away stuck energy. I take my stones and crystals outside so that they can be re-energized by the rain, the wind, the pale winter Sun and the light of the Full Moon.

I open all the windows and invite in the Spirit of Air. I ring chimes all around the room, particularly in the corners, where energy can become stuck. I picture the energy

breaking up and dissipating into the clear pure notes
of the chime bars.

I light a new candle and welcome in the Spirit of Fire!
I dedicate the candle to the Spirit of Transformation! To
resting in the Dark! To regeneration and rebirth! I change
round the furniture, make a new nest for the winter, put
away what I have finished with and bring out what I wish
to explore.

Finally, I go out into the garden and find the last few
flowers and seedheads of the old year to bring in and enjoy.

When all is done, my room feels so different, so
clear and restful. I meditate easily and connect to the
stillness within.

Then I create a new shrine to help myself to focus
on my spiritual path and what I wish to transform. I use a
beautiful dark blue cloth, place on it the sandstone egg I
found near the spring, crystals that I am working with, the
flowers from the garden and light candles. It is very simple
and I like this. I breathe in the Spirit of the Dark and enjoy
the clarity of my space.

Over the next week or two I focus on the death of the
old, the completion of cycles, on endings. In every ending I see
a new beginning. Their death is their rebirth, and this is the
alchemical energy of Samhain.

I keep my feet firmly on the ground, finding pleasure in
simple tasks and acts of kindness, learning not to rush, but
to enjoy each moment for what it is.

I arrange to meet up with friends on a regular basis and we walk in the hills and the woods, in the rain, the mud, the wild wet winds, the sleet and the snow. These walks, where the elements are strong, are the most invigorating! They make us feel alive and strong! They make us laugh with the pure wild joy of being out in the elements!

Symbols of Earth

The Cross

The equal-sided cross is an ancient symbol of the Earth. The four arms represent the Four Elements of Life.

The older symbol of the cross within a circle adds the Fifth Element, representing the Unity and connective force of Spirit and the cyclic nature of all Life.

The Pentacle

The pentacle represents the interconnected Five Elements of Earth, Air, Fire, Water and Spirit. The Pythagorean mystics called it Pent alpha, the birth letter interlaced five times, symbolizing Life and good health.

To the Pagan Celts the pentacle was associated with the Dark Goddess and the womb, the sacred temple of Life, the primal ground of creation where the secret key to all things lay hidden. It was used as a symbol of protection because of its construction from a single unbroken line.

It was also known as the Star of Knowledge and Hermetic magicians used it for their model of Man the Microcosm within the Macrocosm. The pentacle was placed inside a circle representing the cosmos and Unity of Life and inside the pentacle itself was placed a human figure with the feet, hands and head touching each of the points of the pentacle with the genitals at the centre.

The Snake, the Serpent, the Dragon and the Kundalini Serpent

The serpent is an example of an alchemical symbol that is resurfacing after years of being underground, banished and discredited by the Church in an attempt to suppress its ancient power. For thousands of years, the snake, the serpent, the Kundalini serpent and the Dragon were honoured as symbols of the Life Force, regeneration and rebirth. They were symbols of healing energy, creative power and spiritual understanding associated with wisdom and knowledge.

The serpent, the snake, the worm and the Earth Dragon represent the active Life Force flowing through the land. Earth energy travels along energetic pathways linking ancient sacred sites, sacred wells, churches, sacred groves, tumuli and other places of special energy. These are places in the landscape where we can access other parts of ourselves, transcend beyond this plane or enter into other dimensions or other realities. Time runs differently in these places. Our folk traditions are full of altered states and unexpected shifts in Time and the landscape that lead into other dimensions. Many of these folk stories play on our fear of this and effectively block our positive response to these altered states. This can be naturally unlocked by wonder, stillness, receptivity, respect and gratitude.

The Kundalini serpent represents the Life Force in our body and the power of our personal Chi, which is flowing through our chakras. When our chakras are open, the Kundalini flows freely, energizing the health and well-being of our body. Our chakras become closed when we become disconnected from parts of ourselves. The doorways or openings between the chakras become closed through anger, resentment, hurt feelings, suffering and disconnection from the essential Unity of Life. Then the Kundalini serpent cannot enter, cannot energize and cannot flow. The energy becomes blocked, it festers round and round in its own disharmony and the body becomes sick. Understood in this way, this ancient serpent symbol becomes a symbol of freedom, healing, Love and Unity.

The Life Force is released by any act of unification and Love. Universal Love creates openness, which is why the Kundalini is also associated with sacred Love-making. In alchemy it becomes the Ouroboros, the serpent that swallows its own tail (see page 103), a symbol of wholeness and harmony as all becomes One and the Life Force is free to transcend to a new level.

November 9th

Earthing Future Intentions

Tonight we Elementals journey for a vision of 'healing for the Earth' and to ask for our personal direction in this. We decide to journey together using a technique that we have adapted from a Norse shamanic practice using sound to invoke the journey and a staff to anchor the experience.

I have some crystals that I found on the ground in Wales. Their energy feels strong and connected to the Earth and our island. We light a candle and place a basket of the crystals and the candle at the centre of our circle. It is good to sit together, to enjoy the peacefulness of this moment, to breathe deeply and let go of our busy days, our busy minds, letting our energy drop down, down, down into the stillness of the Earth beneath us. We each choose a crystal to take with us on the journey, extending our awareness to join with the energy of the crystal.

We stand in our circle, holding our staffs and crystals, and we each say our intention aloud, so that we are clear when we begin: 'A vision of healing for the Earth and my direction in this.'

We connect to each of the Five Elements in turn, singing, toning and whispering our connection to each one, letting our notes, sounds and words blend and overlap with each other in waves of sounds and images, creating a circle of energy around us and within us.

We then begin the journey by continuing to hum and tone together as we each set off in our mind's eye, each on our own journey, intuitively following the pathways of the imagination that begin to reveal themselves. We sing throughout the journey, as we experience the unfolding world within ourselves…

We each have our own visual images that we use as our entrance to the Otherworld. I picture myself walking down a path in the woods to go down my usual tunnel. But each time I enter the tunnel I keep finding myself back outside. I just can't seem to be able to go down the tunnel in the usual way. I try three times to go down and each time I am back outside. I stand there feeling lost and wonder where I am meant to be if not here. Then suddenly I am flying high over the Earth on the back of a large white eagle! Overview!

The eagle and I travel over many different landscapes and then I find myself looking down on many women, of all nations, cultures and colours. They are looking up and crying out, 'No more!' They are crying and wailing about all the injustices in the world, all the suffering on the Earth. They are crying for those who are hungry and have no clean water to drink, for the polluted waters of our Earth, for the cutting down of the great forests and the terrible chemicals that are being used on the land and are in the food that is being given to the children to eat and the water that they are being given to drink. It is a powerful image of women expressing their feelings openly, women releasing their deep sorrow and deep fury. I join with them. I feel deep sorrow for the lack of care for our Earth and I also feel the rising of power and resolve to create a new future for the Earth.

Then I have a wonderful image of women linking arms together and singing together, united in Spirit, part of a change of heart.

Then I am 'told' – not a voice, but I somehow hear it inside myself – 'Ask for the help of the Angels and the Guardian Spirits.' And as this washes over me, I know that we are not alone, that we have the help of the Angels and Guardian Spirits if we ask them for it.

In the final image of the journey, I am hovering over the Statue of Liberty. It looks like an Angel with a halo. I don't know what this image means, but I know I must remember it and work with it. It is very strong and the journey ends there. I try to move on, to fly on, but this image stays. The journey is over.

We had all agreed before we started our journeys that when they were over we would tone a single note quietly, without variation, to let the others know that we were finished. Now I tone my note and wait until everyone is toning their single note together.

From this 'in-between place', not fully back in normal reality, we each recount our journey. We do this separately, each earthing our journey through song and words.

Then, when we have all shared our journeys, we let out our sounds and sing ourselves back into the present moment and present reality. We pass round some food and spring water, sharing our insights and support for each other. We pledge to take our crystals out and bury them in the Earth as we make a commitment to our vision.

We thank the Five Elements and our Spirit Guides and express our gratitude for the gifts of our journey.

The next day I take my crystal out to my Fire circle in the garden. First I get in touch with all I am feeling about our Western civilization's lack of care for the Earth. We are destroying the very elements of Life upon which we depend, as we pollute our air, our water, our food, our Earth. Collectively, we have come so far from the belief in the interconnected Unity of Life that we have disconnected ourselves from the very Essence of Life itself, the very thing that gives Life to our Soul and meaning to our existence.

As I hold the crystal, I reaffirm that there are no 'us and them', only 'we'. We are the source of change in the world and working together we will make a difference.

I decide not to bury the crystal out of sight but place it on the earth so that when I see it I will remember my journey. I hold the images of my journey in my heart, open up my connection to the Angels and the Guardian Spirits of the Earth and ask for their help in creating beneficial changes for the future.

I light a candle from the Peace Flame pilot light, gather some twigs and autumn leaves from around the garden and light a fire in my ritual Fire circle. I reaffirm my commitment to world Peace and also to inner Peace, aware that this too is linked to the healing of the Earth. I send these thoughts out into Spirit to begin their journey into manifestation.

November 22nd

My Cauldron of Regeneration

I sit in my darkened room and rest in the peaceful stillness that wraps itself around me. Everything in me is shut down, empty, and I am held by the Dark, floating, drifting between the worlds and dreaming new dreams.

I travel into the Darkness, seeing only with my inner eyes as I breathe into my Root chakra in the base of my spine. I feel my Life Spirit, my Chi, anchored to the Earth and anchored in me. It is strong and still and connected to all the threads of my life and to the Web of all Life.

This is my Cauldron of Regeneration, here inside me. I am Life and death united and whole. This is my deepest Union, and I am my own regenerative force, my own rebirth. This is my song, here in the Dark. The pulse of Life is strong in me. The pulse of my Life Force joins with the pulse of the Earth, the pulse of renewal in the Dark, this timeless potency, this Web of Life.

Reflecting the world above, I grow roots down into the Earth, down through the soil and composting vegetation. I join with root and stone, rocks, crystal and bones. I touch the hidden caves and underground waters that are under the Earth and inside me. I send my awareness out to touch the bones of my Ancestors and sacred kin. I send my awareness to meet the spirits of my descendants, and stand on the bridge between the worlds. The connections and bonds of past, present and future meet here in this timeless place.

I am One in this moment and all things are connected. I am One with the nameless seeds within me. I am potential and power, waiting, complete in its Unity and wholeness. I wait, grounded and balanced, touching the Matrix of all possibilities.

HERMES MERCURIUS

Hermes Mercurius leads the way through the Dark. S/he is the Silver Lady, Lady Alchymia, shining her lamp in the darkness. S/he is the archetype inside me and s/he holds up the mirror so that I can see myself reflecting back to myself what I am feeling. How I react in each moment is a perfect reflection of who I am on the inside. This helps me to become aware of what needs to be transformed.

Hermes Mercurius leads me out of the Darkness and into the Light, from the deepest depths to the highest vantage point so that from this overview I gain new perspectives and insights. It is a journey that I can only make for myself. It is a journey of self-discovery, of experiencing all my feelings, both the good and the difficult. Each time I am challenged, Hermes Mercurius holds up the mirror. This shows me a great deal about myself. I thank Hermes Mercurius for this, for without challenges, without being tested, I cannot grow. When I am tested I may be thrown into chaos, but I am offered the opportunity of strengthening my understanding of myself,

of finding equilibrium, healing and inner Peace.

Inner Peace reflects a loyalty to one's self. This means there is never a gap between thought, speech and action. Inner Peace means Peace-with-Self and everything grows from here.

Hermes Mercurius inspires me to unite with all of myself so that I become whole, accepting the Dark as well as the Light. I am learning to transcend them both and rest in the still point between the two.

The gift of rebirth is always with me, in each and every moment. This is the gift of Hermes Mercurius, bringer of revelation and inner wisdom. This is the inspiration s/he brings me, the vision to heal myself from the inside so that I am free to move on and begin the new.

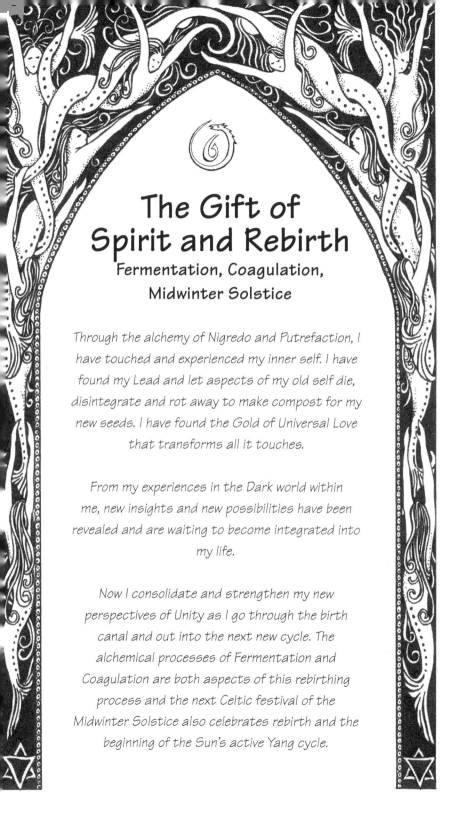

The Gift of
Spirit and Rebirth
Fermentation, Coagulation,
Midwinter Solstice

Through the alchemy of Nigredo and Putrefaction, I
have touched and experienced my inner self. I have
found my Lead and let aspects of my old self die,
disintegrate and rot away to make compost for my
new seeds. I have found the Gold of Universal Love
that transforms all it touches.

From my experiences in the Dark world within
me, new insights and new possibilities have been
revealed and are waiting to become integrated into
my life.

Now I consolidate and strengthen my new
perspectives of Unity as I go through the birth
canal and out into the next new cycle. The
alchemical processes of Fermentation and
Coagulation are both aspects of this rebirthing
process and the next Celtic festival of the
Midwinter Solstice also celebrates rebirth and the
beginning of the Sun's active Yang cycle.

The Alchemical Experience of Fermentation

Fermentation grows out of the Putrefaction process and chemically is the growth of a ferment (bacteria), which brings the growth of new Life. For the alchemist, the experience of Fermentation brings new energy and new ways forward. Out of the regenerative Dark come new realizations, meaningful visions, rebirth and inspiration from within or from the 'Above'.

In alchemy this rebirth is known as 'the Peacock's Tail' or 'the Rainbow Bridge', which joins the 'Above' with the 'Below', uniting our spiritual path with our future actions. The Rainbow Bridge is a symbol of living inspiration from within us and beyond us, and is seen as a resurrection or rebirth into a new level of understanding.

New Life is now rising with the Life Force, the inner serpent, the living energy of Life. It is re-energized by the return of Yang Fire, Sol, the Sun, activating the watery inner world and bringing the inspiration to move out of the Dark.

I experience Fermentation as a re-energizing of my outer path through my deepest visions and the seeds of change that are stirring within me. I feel ready to move again, to take action, to activate new paths forward. I bring with me my connection to Spirit and all that I have learned from the inner journey. Through Fermentation I experience rebirth, moving on and moving outwards through the creation of new possibilities from within.

The Alchemical Experience of Coagulation

Coagulation brings strengthening and consolidation. Chemically, the liquids and gases from Putrefaction begin to solidify. This is transformation from a fluid state into a solid state. During Putrefaction the Lead has been broken down to its base components and when it eventually coalesces again, it is cleansed of all impurities and a glimpse of the alchemist's Gold can be seen.

Alchemically, Coagulation represents what we bring into rebirth, what we make solid, what we move out of the fluid state of infinite possibilities into the solid state of manifestation.

Here, Water is at its height and re-energises the conscious mind to actively move out of the inner pathways into outer action. This stage is known as the return of Sol and Fire. Coagulation is the development of spiritual strength and taking this strength out into the world. It is time to make choices that will refine and strengthen our connection to our spiritual path.

In alchemy this is symbolized by the creation of an egg or seed with a glimpse of the Gold inside. The inner and outer worlds are joined in one continuous circuit, also symbolized by the Ouroboros, the serpent with its tail in its mouth (*see page 103*). Everything is connected: the Dark and the Light, 'Within and Without', 'Above and Below', Spirit and Matter.

My strength lies in integrating the insights and realizations gained on my inner journey into my daily life, thereby keeping these understandings alive and actively part of my development. This creates new ways forward, a rebirth, strengthened by the rising power of Spirit from within and the roots of true goodness and integrity.

The Alchemy of Spirit

In alchemy, Spirit is called Quintessence, the Fifth Element, the quintessential limitless energy of Life, the abundant Essence of All Things, the Source of All Things, the open circuit through which all things are united. Spirit is Unity – complete, harmonious, inclusive Unity. It is the alchemist's maxim 'As Above, so Below', Spirit in Matter, joined as One. For in Spirit there is no separation, only streams of vibrational energy – Infinite, boundless energy.

We are all Spirit, all the time, always. In this sense there is no separation between Life and death, no here and there, no Time, no duality or polarity. Spirit is Oneness, instant, eternal, total integration, never still but always One, always becoming yet never changing.

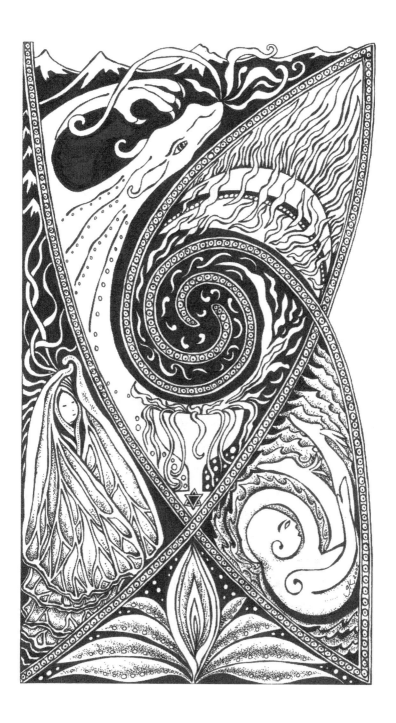

Spirit is the connecting force. In Spirit there is no beginning and no end. There is continuation, the continuous cycles of creation. I create vibrations in Spirit with my every thought, word and action, and whatever I do comes back to me. It is not who I am or what I am that is important, it is what I add to the vibrational streams all around me. This creates what I bring into being and what I bring to the whole.

My inner journey has brought me a deeper understanding of this, and the more I integrate it into my life, the more I experience it and the more my connection to Spirit is strengthened.

The Alchemy of the Midwinter Solstice

The Midwinter Solstice marks the end of the waning cycle of the Sun and the fullness of the Yin cycle. It is the darkest part of the year, the shortest day and the longest night. This falls between December 20th and 23rd in the Northern Hemisphere and June 20th and 23rd in the Southern Hemisphere. It marks the end of the Yin cycle and the beginning of the Yang cycle (see chart on page 27).

The Earth's cycle is kept in harmonious equilibrium by the waxing and waning cycle of the Sun, creating the balanced forces of Yin and Yang. At Midsummer, the element of Fire, the active force, energized the element of Water, the receptive force, and this took me on a journey within. Now, at Midwinter, it is the element of Water that energizes Fire to bring action, so that inspiration from within can become manifest.

The Midwinter Solstice is a celebration of the return of the Sun, the return of the Light and the return of the outer growth cycle. From now on the days will slowly become longer and lighter and the Sun warmer. After rest and regeneration in the Dark, the Earth is once again preparing for new growth, ready to express the fertility and abundance of Life.

As with Midsummer Solstice, this is a dual celebration and I value and celebrate both the Dark and the Light as important parts of the whole. I look forward to the new possibilities that the new cycle will bring and I look back to celebrate the inner journey. I name and honour what I have achieved, what I have let go of and what has been transformed.

The Midwinter Solstice is a moment of rebirth when I activate what I choose to bring out into my life and into the Light. Solstice means 'Standing of the Sun' and this is a moment to stand still and stay in the moment. I stand at the great doorway between the inner growth cycle and the outer growth cycle and ask, 'What do I want to do? What do I wish to grow? What is my golden egg of rebirth? What energy do I wish to carry through into the year's new cycle?'

As the energy moves outwards once again, I aim to keep connected to my Inner Realms during the new growth season.

The time for action has not yet come, but in the stillness I look for the alchemy, the changes I can make in my life, the things that would make a difference. I don't want to rush into things that I can't sustain, so as well as keeping hold of the bigger picture, I concentrate on what is manageable and sustainable in my life right now. This reduces stress and ensures a greater chance of real success. As I move into this new phase, I bring out the Gold that has been revealed in the Dark, my realization that Universal Love is the transformative Gold I wish to work with consciously and purposefully.

I feel like a snake shedding its skin as I leave behind old ways of being, old patterns, old parts of myself, and reach out for the new. My awareness of the Unity and interconnectedness of the Web of Life is strengthened. I am aware of the aspects of myself that have held me back in the past and I am determined to leave these behind.

As part of my active rebirth I name new seeds, new intentions – my resolutions for the new cycle. I nurture these inside myself, in my heart and in my mind, earthing them in the practical changes I begin to make.

The vibration in which these new seeds are planted sets them in motion. It is this that attracts what they need to grow. So I meditate with this awareness and create an alchemical moment as I unite past, present and future into One, picturing what I wish to bring in as whole and complete and happening now. I do not need to know how it will be achieved, only have the certainty that it will. I reach for my dreams and remove any limiting thoughts of what is possible and what is impossible.

This isn't easy! Every day I confront my negative voice, the voice that limits me and blocks the flow to my abundance. I take these doubts, accept that they are part of me and then set about reversing their destructive energy. Once again I use the alchemy of Separation and Union and the transformative power of Universal Love to transform the old. So I take every negative statement that I hear myself making and replace it with a positive statement. I say the positive statement often – whenever I remember, first thing in the morning and last thing at night, and especially when I find myself reverting back to the old familiar negative patterns. Eventually, the new positive statement becomes established, the old patterns of negative response begin to stop and I know that I am making real progress.

I embrace the certainty that all my positive and loving actions are helping to change my life for the better and are bringing more positivity, Peace and Love into the world.

I use this time at the Midwinter Solstice to activate my 'Yes!' to fire up the Love in my heart and bring to birth positive loving solutions for myself and for the world. When I choose loving solutions, whether in my personal life or on a world scale, the door opens to positive change and healing. Everything I do makes a difference. I use my power as a consumer to buy products that support fair trade, renewable energy, sustainability, recycling and organic farming. I support ethical businesses, ethical banking and ethical trade. Each one of my purchases increases the availability of these things.

This is my 'Yes!' and my inner truth, and I support my truth with every choice I make.

I activate appreciation as one of my rebirthing solutions. Appreciation makes my heart sing! I appreciate all I have right now and I am filled up, I have so much! I use appreciation to dispel dissatisfaction and resentment and to balance any feelings of lack or unworthiness. Appreciation for the positive increases the positive and opens the door to its abundance in the world and in my life.

December 20th

The Celebrations Group

The Celebrations Group is a group of local friends who have been meeting to celebrate the Celtic festivals for many years now. We all live within a 20-mile radius of one another and yet we are a community and family who have shared our lives and supported each other as our children have grown from toddlers to teenagers. We take it in turns to host and plan each celebration, sometimes in our homes or out in the local countryside, or sometimes we hire a village hall and share the cost.

Every year we put on a much larger event to celebrate the Midwinter Solstice and this has now become a local tradition. We hire a large village hall and set the scene for a true community gathering with all our local friends and their families co-creating a very special and heart-warming day. The hall is decked with greenery, hangings and creations that people have made. We create a ceremony and our own entertainment, music and dancing. Everyone contributes and everyone brings food and drink so that we share a great feast together and presents for a present share. These we put in baskets labelled 'Child', 'Teen' or 'Adult' and they are shared out at the end.

This year Ros has made two large Angels out of willow, tissue paper and fabric. She calls them the Dark Angel and the Light Angel. They are quite large and hold nightlights inside them so they light up from the inside. We hang them in opposite corners of the room, with material behind them. They look wonderful and their presence reminds us that we are poised on this threshold between the Dark and the Light.

The celebration begins with a fantastic drumming and percussion session. Everyone joins in, from accomplished djembe players to two-year-olds shaking rattles. Our teenagers plug in their electric guitars and jam along too. It is a great fusion of generations and styles, a true tribal moment. There is a wonderful sense of connection as we all play together and I feel as if my heart will burst with happiness. This is family! This is community!

Gradually the high energy subsides and we gather into a circle, holding hands around a single candle in a large bowl of sand with evergreens around it and a basket of nightlights beside it. It looks so beautiful, so peaceful and still in the silence. We sing a gentle Solstice chant, harmonizing with each other, letting the notes and sounds rise and fall and weave together.

After connecting to the Earth beneath us and the stars above us, and acknowledging the Five Elements, we devise a ceremony together. We decide that when each person is ready, they will light a candle and take it to the Dark Angel with gratitude for their journey through the dark of the year or to the Light Angel with their hopes and visions for the new year about to begin.

We all hold sacred space for each other, gently humming as everyone lights their candles and places them with the Dark and Light Angels and says what they want to say. It is very heart-warming and moving – so much gratitude, so much Love for the Earth and her people, for each other and for ourselves. Many people light several candles, and candles are also put into the bowl of sand at the centre to acknowledge the Dark and the Light together.

Gradually the room becomes filled with light!

We take up our chant again and before long it transforms into a new energy and a new drumming and dancing session is under way. Then we bring the food in, set up tables and have a great feast. This is followed by entertainment – singing, music, performances and plays that everyone contributes to, both children and adults.

I leave with my heart bursting with Love for my friends and my community. With simplicity and goodwill, with everyone contributing something, we have created a beautiful occasion to mark this point of transition in the Earth's cycle. We have honoured what has passed and have opened the door to new beginnings, and this day lives on in all our hearts.

I take many gifts with me through the Solstice doorway. I take this Love for my friends and my local community. I take gratitude for my family and my teenage children. I am filled with appreciation of the simple pleasures in life, my home and my friendships. I take with me the realization that it is the Love in my heart that matters the most to me. It is the Love in my heart that makes me feel happy and full of well-being. It is the Love in my heart that lives on, and this is what I rebirth into the new growth cycle. This is my Gold.

December 22nd
A Journey to the Kings Oak

Here at the Midwinter Solstice I make a journey in my mind's eye back to the Kings Oak that I visited at the Midsummer Solstice. I make myself comfortable in my darkened room and play a shamanic drumming CD (see Appendix, page 269). Because I know the physical landscape so well from all the times I have been in this field, I have a clear picture and instantly feel that I am there.

It is very quiet here now, the stone circle standing silent and still. Only a few birds are active, flitting about in the trees and hedgerows, bringing the only movement and sound in the sleeping landscape. It feels so good to return here at the heart of the winter. The mighty Kings Oak tree stands in its stillness, its branches bare of leaves, the pulse of its Life Force so low now, so deep within the Earth.

I greet the tree deeply and gently and once again sit at the interface where the tree's huge root system disappears below ground. I am conscious again of the message from the Oak given to me at the Midsummer Solstice. It has been within me throughout my journey as I have searched for what truly inspires me.

Time and again I have experienced and understood that the thing that truly inspires me is the Love in my heart. When I am touched by this Love, this central core of my Unity, I am happy; when I lose touch with it, I am unhappy.

I sit and meditate with this understanding, which the Midwinter Solstice and the Fermentation and Coagulation experience have strengthened. I find myself merging with the pulse of the tree, deep inside the Earth, aware of the Earth's energy waiting to turn outwards and upwards once again.

I breathe in the stillness of Midwinter, feeling the deep strength and stability of my inner stillness. I earth this in my inner Philosopher's Stone, so that I can *reconnect to this moment again, anchoring it in my heart as it blends with my joy and the Love already there.*

December 31st
The Return of Fire

I am learning to trust my feelings and act on the inspiration that comes from within, on the moments of illogical clarity and spontaneous action. Synchronicity is everywhere in a delightful expression of alchemy and Unity, as my inner and outer worlds merge. It is present in every perfect moment, in every joy, in the things that ring true or manifest unexpectedly. It is there in every loving positive action, in acts of kindness and goodwill, in my spontaneous choices that reflect my inner Peace and express Unity. I don't always get it right, but I know when I do, and this is what I build on.

I activate my renewed connection to Fire and become the Phoenix, the Firebird, rising from the ashes of Nigredo and Putrefaction with a raised awareness of the Unity within me. I become the Salamander, strengthened by my journey in the Dark, bringing new insights and new visions from a deeper understanding of myself. Like the Salamander I choose to live in both the inner world and the outer world at the same time. My actions are inspired from within, from my connection to my spiritual path, sparked by my intuition, by my passion and by my Love.

I am aware that I have choices and what I choose to do right now will shape the future. I am aware that I can consciously make the choices that will draw towards me the things that I want. So, what are my new intentions, new directions and new paths? I think about this a lot at this time and buy a large gold candle and use it as the focus for my Gold.

I light the candle from the Peace Flame still alchemically held in the pilot light of the boiler and I say: 'For Peace Within and Peace Without. To integrate my spiritual path with all I do in my everyday life.'

I know that it is the Love in my heart that keeps the door open to my inner Peace and links my inner spirituality with what I do in life. This Universal Love creates loving responses and loving actions. When I perceive Spirit as Love and Unity in all things, that is what I receive. Spirit reflects back to me whatever I project onto it.

I stare into the candle flame, keeping focused on this, opening the channels to my internal fluidity and the place of all possibilities.

I light a pink candle from the gold candle and make a new affirmation: 'To follow my most loving response.' I meditate with this for a while, letting my mind unite with this idea, sensing how this will transform everything I do and respond to. I have a memory of the inner journey vision of the women crying together and then linking arms in co-operation, and I unite this with my seed to follow my most loving response. I create an open channel to this vision, knowing that it will manifest in the future if I keep the circuit alive and open.

I light another candle, a rainbow one: 'For my commitment to join with others, especially women, to activate the power of our Love to make a difference in the world.'

Leading on from this, I remember the rest of that journey. I was to ask for help from the Angels and Guardians. So I choose a simple white candle and light it: 'For the Angels, Spirit Guides and Guardians of the Earth. Please help those who are doing their best to help the Earth.'

Now I have three candles burning around my central gold candle, three seeds of Gold that I have planted, brought to Life by my thoughts, by the lighting of the candles and by the words I have spoken. I leave them to burn for a while and then send my pledges and intentions out on the Spirit of Air as I blow them out. This means I can relight them to reaffirm the links I have made today.

January 10th
Planting Seeds of Gold

I plant some Thyme seeds to grow inside on the window ledge. Thyme is used energetically to bring courage, inner strength and strong purpose. I need all of these qualities and initiate their energy in myself as I plant the seeds in the compost. In the spring I will use these Thyme plants as part of a Peace bower I want to create in my garden, a peaceful place to sit, a focus for my thoughts on Peace. As I plant the seeds I activate the seed intentions I made to keep them in my thoughts.

I am aware that the energetic seeds I plant now will unite with the new growth cycle of the Earth. My personal seeds, my seeds of Gold, are my potential for new growth and development in the coming cycle, as the warmth returns and daylight increases.

I want to build bridges that link my inner world to my actions in the outer world, so that my spiritual journey is part of my everyday life. I picture throwing a long golden thread from my inner world to aspects of my everyday life, joining the two together as one. So I strengthen the links that join the two parts of myself together.

I hold this vision of my integrated self as I embrace new beginnings and the birth of a new cycle. I am conscious of the power of my words, my thoughts and actions. I am conscious that my inner Peace is reflected out and adds to the stream of Peace that is available in the world. I am conscious of the way that my loving awareness and loving responses are changing my life and creating positive actions that hold the potential for great transformation. I don't always get it right; I can still find myself reacting from resentment and fear of lack. But each time I experience my disconnection from Love and Unity I bring myself back by developing strategies that use Love as the catalyst to return me to my centre.

I am beginning to see anything that throws me offcentre as a gift and I am learning to catch these disconnections and use them as trigger points to transform the negative by replacing it quickly with the positive. This way I change irritability into good humour, worries into trust, resentment into appreciation. I follow the things that strengthen my Life Force, my Chi, and stop doing the things that drain me.

January 28th

Lighting Candles Day

It's so damp and dark these days and it's raining outside again. I light the fire so that soon I am transformed from feeling miserable to feeling cosy and content. I light my big gold candle and the remains of my three pledge-candles.

I say my affirmations and pledges as I light them and sit and watch them in a very mercurial state of being. I let my thoughts, heart and Spirit merge as I drift in and out of a meditative daydream state, breathing in my contentment and simply being, sitting and resting.

I light another candle with deep appreciation for my life and for the gift of gratitude that helps me to transform my experiences into a positive vibration that opens doorways to my inner happiness. Before long I have lit lots of candles and nightlights and dedicated them to people I love – to both of my parents, to my children and partner, to friends and sacred kin – and to new dreams, to healing, to new ways forward. The room is filled with candlelight and the joy of this celebratory alchemical moment! Each candle has brought a connection, a renewal of Love.

I sit for a long time by the fire, reflecting, staring into space, enjoying the flickering warmth of so many candle flames, watching the rain pour down outside. And then I suddenly feel inspired to gather up all the crystals, rocks and stones from the window ledges and baskets and take them out into the rain. As I lay them out on the wall outside, I remember where each one came from, connecting them in my mind to people and places in the past. I feel them come alive through my contact with them and their return to the elements!

I reconnect to the egg-shaped stone from the spring, the stone I have been using in my meditations to anchor my understandings, feelings, insights and my growing awareness of the alchemy of Love and Unity. I am aware of how these have been refined and strengthened by my journey through the winter. This is my Philosopher's Stone united within me. I have anchored my precious Gold inside myself so that it is always ready to draw on whenever I need it. I thank the stone for its help at the beginning of this process and next time I go to the spring I will put it back into the fastflowing stream.

It's very refreshing to be out in the rain and I set off walking fast to generate some inner Fire against the cold and wet. I feel changed by my morning's experiences. I have experienced a great Oneness with all of Life around me. I breathe this into myself as I walk, earthing it into the Philosopher's Stone inside me. I feel all joined up, connected on the outside to inside, to my past, to this present moment and through my seed intentions to my future.

HERMES MERCURIUS

Hermes Mercurius travels between the worlds and is the great bridge-builder uniting Spirit and Matter. Neither solid nor liquid, neither female nor male, s/he is indefinable, a free spirit, unconfined and mutable. In a meditation, Hermes Mercurius tells me not to follow my mind but to follow my heart. This makes sense to me when I trust the Love in my heart as the guide for my mind. My fluidity, spontaneity and my freedom of speech and action depend on this conscious awareness of being led by the Love in my heart.

I become like Hermes Mercurius as I build a bridge across the great divides of Spirit and Matter. I join the two together and they fit comfortably together inside me. This fundamental Unity opens the door to more Unity. This is more of the alchemist's Gold that I have experienced on this journey. The more Unity I experience, the stronger it becomes.

I am struck by the power that Unity has for healing the great social, political, religious and psychological divides, the separations and dualistic thinking that

have ruled our world for such a long time, the multitude of polarities that have held us back from this truth. Unity creates a common bond that instantly creates Peace and healing.

I am inspired by the thought that Hermes Mercurius, Spirit of communication, is in her element in this present Age. Telephones, television, mobile phones, the Internet and e-mails are all instant forms of communication, and this means we are sharing information, visions and actions worldwide. We are no longer cut off from each other, but united. Potentially everything is out in the open and potentially we are connected to virtual communities of like-minded people. This opens up the possibility of energy sharing as we create a web of power through our united vision of 'One World, One Family'. We can all tap into this and gain strength from our collective energy.

When we send an e-mail, make a phone call or write a letter, our feelings and our thoughts are sent as well. They are energetically joined together with the other form of communication. I think of my thoughts as links, energy pathways of communication. Each time I throw a thought out, a line of

communication opens. If I have the thought enough times, the link strengthens and becomes like a well-used pathway, an open channel, 'a line open'.

Hermes Mercurius makes no distinction between good and bad, for this is just another polarity. The myth tells us that s/he is a slippery character, a trickster, not always trusted by the gods. S/he would change the message on the way or have some fun at their expense. Our minds can play tricks on us and our own thoughts cannot always be trusted. I can become polarized, full of comparisons and dualistic thinking, and then all my hard-won harmony and Unity is gone! I understand Hermes Mercurius as a tester, helping me to strengthen my inner truth, which comes from deep within.

Hermes Mercurius is the alchemist, pushing the boundaries and holding up the separated parts so that they are seen and not hidden, and then joining them together again. This is the alchemist's strength and it lies in the desire to change and to grow, to transform through the power of Unity.

Hermes Mercurius inspires me to

look to the next stage, to refine this ability, to transfigure from our old state of being into a new vibration of Oneness and Unity. From here it is possible to be able to change a substance or form — the alchemist's ultimate aim of the transmutation of Matter. Here lies the key to healing and to realigning energy, to neutralizing pollution within ourselves and in the outer world. I am willing to be open to this possibility, so the doorway is open and the Life Force flows through to give it Life.

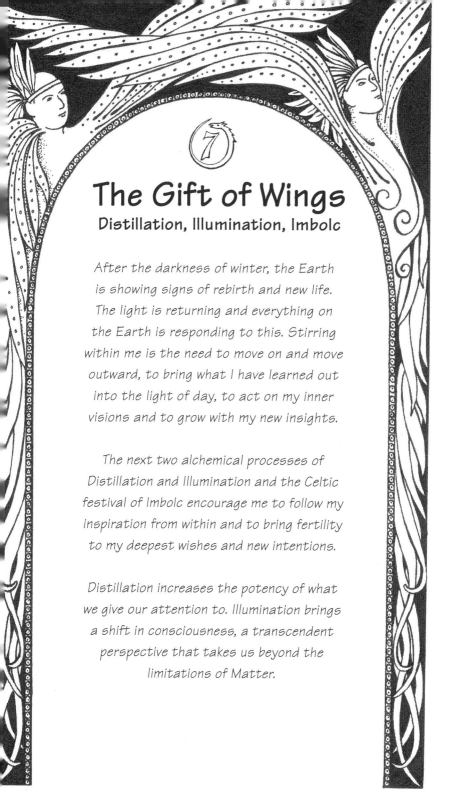

⑦ The Gift of Wings

Distillation, Illumination, Imbolc

After the darkness of winter, the Earth
is showing signs of rebirth and new life.
The light is returning and everything on
the Earth is responding to this. Stirring
within me is the need to move on and move
outward, to bring what I have learned out
into the light of day, to act on my inner
visions and to grow with my new insights.

The next two alchemical processes of
Distillation and Illumination and the Celtic
festival of Imbolc encourage me to follow my
inspiration from within and to bring fertility
to my deepest wishes and new intentions.

Distillation increases the potency of what
we give our attention to. Illumination brings
a shift in consciousness, a transcendent
perspective that takes us beyond the
limitations of Matter.

The Alchemical Experience of Distillation

Distillation represents the raising of Spirit, the reenergizing of Life from within. Chemically, it is the boiling and condensation of the fermented solution to increase its purity, as in the distillation of wine to make brandy. It rises up and runs back down the sides of the flask in continuous cycles, linking everything together, refining and transforming. In alchemy it is the linking of the 'Above' and the 'Below', energizing, strengthening and refining through experience and endless cycles.

The alchemical symbols associated with Distillation are the Infinity symbol, the Ouroboros and the circle (see page 103). The experience of Distillation encourages us to think in cyclic motion, going beyond linear duality and into an awareness of all Life as circulating energy.

The Distillation experience generates wisdom from within, which circulates into all our actions. This returns to us as more wisdom and rises up again to circulate new ideas and actions. Distillation creates circuits of connected energy.

The Eastern alchemists called Distillation 'Circulating the Light' and linked it to enlightenment, the realization of Unconditional Love. It is also linked to the awakening of Kundalini energy, the repeated raising of the Life Force, which unites the chakras (see page 259) so that good health is reflected into the body from the inside.

Distillation helps me to refine and purify my understanding and intentions. This means that the seeds of my Gold become clearer each time I engage with them and I develop a deeper relationship with my spiritual path. I use meditation, contemplation and visualization to help my ideas to come to the surface and to help me to see where I am going. They are made stronger each time they rise up inside me and activate my actions in the physical world. Everything is a reflection and refining of this balance of Spirit in Matter. What is within is reflected out into all I do, say and think.

Everything I do that strengthens my spiritual values increases my commitment to them, and although I am just one person, I know that everything I do creates catalysts for changing the bigger picture. There is much in the world that I want to help change and I am inspired by the thought that working together as a community of like-minded people, we can make a real difference in the world. I experience community with my local friends and family and can extend this to my extended family and friends and all the like-minded people in this country and Europe, expanding further into the virtual community of the Internet, which potentially links me to my world family.

I remember that I am also energy and vibration, and it is not only the physical things that I do that create change. My thoughts, prayers, healing, Love and intentions also make a difference to the whole.

Every day I try to make time for my daily practice. This includes meditation, positive affirmations and creating Love, healing and Peace in my life. These are all part of my personal Distillation process, circulating the things I choose to do to support myself and my family in the best way I know how.

For me, as a mother and homemaker, change and alchemy begin at home and spread out from my everyday life into the bigger picture. I support life-enhancing environmental projects, developing my commitment to respecting and preserving the natural environment through the food we eat and the products we buy. This then moves outwards from my small world and adds to the availability of non-abusive methods of farming and medicine and ecologically sustainable industry which supports respect for all Life. I am lucky enough to have this freedom of choice, and I will not waste it.

Now the new growth cycle begins from a place of strong roots and a stable foundation, so that when the inner Fire sparks and the Life Force rises up and sets in motion new ideas, I am able to throw myself into Life with enthusiasm and spontaneity.

The Alchemical Experience of Illumination

Illumination re-activates the element of Air to bring communication and connection with the Spirit Realms, and what is rising from within. This Union with Spirit brings fertility and creativity to the outer world.

In alchemy this is a renewal of consciousness, the raising of Sol, the Sun, the Yang, the conscious active principle, to a new level. This brings new philosophical insights and radiance from within, which in turn leads to unique new solutions, illuminating new ways forward.

The alchemical symbols of Illumination are those of flight: wings, Angels, Spirit Guides, the white swan, the eagle, winged figures, winged creatures, including Hermes Mercurius and the Caduceus. The experience of Illumination is an enlightened state of being, represented in sacred art by an illuminated head or a halo.

The experience of Illumination represents a breakthrough into an exalted state of Bliss, where Spirit shines from within. Mind, body and Spirit are united and there is a shift from self-interest to a desire to add to the greater good and to be of service in the world.

Illumination lights the way to new levels of awareness, to the alchemical transformation of Spirit into Matter. It is an awakening to the radiant inner Light of Spirit, a state of Grace, spiritual Bliss, Heaven on Earth, a transcendent perspective, a shift in perception as the Gold is revealed.

Illumination lifts my awareness. It is rebirth in action as new insights come to the surface and my realizations create lasting transformation from the inside. My spiritual journey guides me now and this creates a change of perspective and a change of focus in how I live my life.

My journey is leading me into a deep awareness of the sacredness of Life, the sacredness of our Earth and the Five Elements. I am moving out of old ways of thinking, moving forward, ready to experience and test this new awareness.

I am open to the flow of Love as an unlimited and unlimiting transformative force of Unity and healing. I activate its fertility and magic as I raise it up and bring it out into my life and into the world.

Chopping Wood and Carrying Water

When I write about all this in this way, it seems so elevated and yet at the same time it resonates as the truth that is inside me. When I remember my higher purpose, I experience this state of Grace. I don't always remember, and the only way I know how to keep remembering is to integrate these higher ideals into my everyday life, to bring them down to Earth so that they (and I) don't float off and become too airy, too elevated and insubstantial.

Much of what I do each day is very ordinary – the cooking, the washing, cleaning, gardening, all the everyday aspects of family life. I remind myself that it is the way in which these things are done that creates the alchemy and a beneficial shift in consciousness.

'Chopping Wood and Carrying Water' is a Zen expression for doing these everyday jobs as a form of meditation, with consciousness and stillness and with the awareness of the sacred in all things. This makes a big difference to me. I learn to slow down, to energetically unite my spirituality with everything I do. It brings me great happiness and harmony from the inside, and it is this that creates the alchemy and change on the outside. My happiness and contentment spread outwards into the way I am living, into my relationships and to my family, spreading out through them and continuing on and on to who knows where.

For Love lights the Fire for more Love in the world. It is a simple truth and one I like to remember often.

Chopping Wood and Carrying Water takes the task beyond the actual job. When the job is a meditation, it is done in a different way. For example, I don't just clean, I space clear (see page 133) and this puts me back in touch with another level of awareness and my internal reality. So Chopping Wood and Carrying Water becomes a way for me to access deeper and more subtle parts of myself. As with all meditation, it allows me to become still enough to become aware of the interconnected Web of Life, to slip beyond Time and experience another way of 'seeing'. Through this state of 'mindfulness', as it is called, I become the observer, aware of what I am thinking and feeling in a more detached way. From this shift in consciousness I am in a better position to make choices and initiate the alchemy and the transformation I want to see happen. Once the chatter in my mind has subsided, I have greater access to my imagination and I am more alert to what is bubbling up from the subtle levels of my being.

In this state I notice a shift towards feelings of gratitude and appreciation for all that I have in this moment. It is there in the beauty that I see all around me, in the shaft of sunlight coming down through the trees, in an unfolding leaf, in light sparkling on the water, in the Robin hopping so expertly in the bush outside my window. It is there in the beauty of people, especially children. It is there in acts of kindness and natural goodness, in spontaneous actions that lift the hearts of others, in the gift of giving and the gift of receiving. Love is everywhere, and when my heart is open, synchronicity happens and I am able to notice it.

Of course I am not always in this state of complete contentment. Some days I am grumpy, irritable, sad and dissatisfied, and I become very disconnected from Unity and Love! Mercurius is there (often in the guise of my teenage children), ready to test me, strengthen my truth, help me to see the triggers that push me off my cloud. Then I have to find my way out of the depths again and reconnect. I look for the Lead that is weighing me down, the Lead that needs transforming, and always there is Gold to be found.

Chopping Wood and Carrying Water helps me to explore the root and the route of the disconnection I am feeling and to reconnect to Spirit and the sacredness of Life. It helps me to put things in order and to put things back into perspective.

As well as getting the menial everyday jobs done, I also work to restore inner harmony.

Many years ago, during a difficult time in my life, I spent many months in a reclusive state, just Chopping Wood and Carrying Water every day until I gradually regained my inner Peace and was able to step back out into the world once again.

I also spend a lot of time Chopping Wood and Carrying Water not as part of a recovery process but simply because there is nothing finer than the simplicity of experiencing this state of 'being', and being filled up from the inside.

Tending the garden is another form of meditation which brings me inner connection. By growing beautiful flowers, food to eat and herbs to use in the kitchen and as medicine, by co-creating with Nature, by working with the Elements and the Earth, I become peaceful and stable from the inside. Creativity, art and craftwork and walks in beautiful places do the same. They are all ways to experience the alchemy of connection to Spirit, Union and transformation from the inside, through the simple pleasures of life.

The Alchemy of Imbolc

In the Northern Hemisphere Imbolc is celebrated around the end of January/beginning of February and in the Southern Hemisphere around the end of July/beginning of August. Imbolc is the Celtic festival that celebrates the awakening Earth. It is linked to the festival of Lammas (see page 62) across the Wheel of the Year (see chart on page 27). Lammas marks the initiation and beginning of the inner journey and Imbolc marks the initiation and beginning of the outer journey. Both are linked to the element of Air, the connective force, which unites and opens the channels between the seen and the unseen, the inner and the outer worlds.

Imbolc alchemy lies in the joining of the inner with the outer, in harnessing receptivity, the intuition and the imagination as active tools for the journey ahead. The alchemy of Imbolc happens in the transference of energy from the inside to the outside, as in the alchemical experience of Distillation.

Imbolc is a celebration of the awakening Earth and the rising Life Force that initiates fertility and growth. The time for action is beginning and Imbolc is a reminder to keep the links to the inner world open, to keep in touch with our intuition and our receptivity to the inner journey, as we go forth into the outer world.

Imbolc has a long tradition of honouring and celebrating creativity of all kinds. In the past, poetry, song, art, all craftwork, especially metalwork and women's crafts such as embroidery and sewing, were all considered to be sacred acts of power, a way of channelling the Inner Mysteries. The creative act was seen as a tool of magic, a way of manifesting what was invoked during the process of creation. This interests me and I become more aware of what I bring to what I am creating through my energy, and what I invoke and consciously activate through my creative work.

Poetry and song were also considered to be ways of tapping into our ancestral memory, which rises from the inner world and can be contacted through the Muse. The Muse is said to whisper inspiration in our ear and I perceive her as another Spirit Guide or Angel figure that brings insight from within me.

It is time to activate my seeds and intentions by giving them attention. I refine and strengthen them with actions that support their growth. I also encourage their growth by daily visualizations and affirmations and by adjusting my thinking to include them as what will surely manifest in the future. I feel clear and certain that they will be there, so I know that on an energetic level their manifestation has already been set in motion.

I remember to keep the channels of communication open so that I receive impressions, insights and communication from the Spirit Realms, from my Spirit Guides and the Angels. In a meditation I receive an image of the Earth as an Angel, her protective wings spread around the globe. I see the Life Force stirring in her as the golden light from the Sun brings her awake. She stretches her wings in the sunlight, renewed and refreshed from her long winter sleep. She is the Fertile Force, the Spirit of the Maiden Goddess, reborn and potent, seeking Union with the Life Force, the serpent force of the land.

The serpent moves out from within the Earth and transforms into the Dragon, and the paths of Earth energy begin to become active again as Nature awakes. In the past, wells and springs were honoured at Imbolc, to celebrate their reactivation and to honour the Life-giving water that comes up from the depths of the Earth, from the Dark into the Light.

The Kundalini serpent force also rises in me. I sense the fertile potency rising and I visualize my chakras opening and uniting as energy and Light circulate inside me. I visualize the movement and interweaving of my vital Life Force and the release of healing energy this reflects out into my life. I celebrate my Chi, my Life Force, and my well-being every day.

I celebrate my relationship with the Earth, with the land around me, and the power of the new growth cycle to bring transformation and change into my life. I celebrate the rising energy of the element Fire, the Sun, and its power to initiate and spark my imagination and my creativity. I celebrate the element of Air and the many levels of communication that are open to me. I celebrate the element of Water and the power of my emotions to move me, to touch my very Soul from within, so that I experience Spirit rising within me.

January 30th
Awakening Earth

I live in a valley, with hills either side. I often sit by my window, looking out at the hills behind our house, simply 'being'.

I sometimes meditate here with my eyes open but unfocused, observing my thoughts washing over me, letting stillness descend, 'Circulating the Light'. The window faces East and through this view I experience the early morning colours and lightening of the dawn sky as it spreads out from behind the hill. I watch sunrises, moonrises, ever-changing cloud formations, rainbows, reflected sunsets, fogs and mists ascending and descending. The hillside has so many different atmospheres. There are always changes to be seen, always delight and wonder to be experienced through the changing seasons, the changing colours of the land, the changing colours and patterns of the light and the changing weather.

I walk in these hills, so as I look out of the window I have the extraordinary experience of having a three-dimensional visual map before me! I see a landscape I can step into, fields, trees and woods that I know, tracks and footpaths, green lanes that I walk along, farmsteads and animals in the fields that I walk by.

For the last week I have noticed one dramatic change in the view of the land: a cluster of Willow trees which were previously just blending in with the other bare winter trees in the landscape have turned a bright golden orange. They are lit up, even on a dull day. Their rising sap has transformed them so that their bark is bright with their changing energy and they are calling me to go and visit!

It is a dull, damp morning but the pull of the Willows is so strong that I set off along the footpaths to go and visit them. The birds' song is really loud, proclaiming that spring is on its way. It's good to see the fresh new green of the Bluebell leaves pushing through the soil and the sense of the aliveness of the awakening Earth is tangible. The first spring flowers – Snowdrops, Primroses, Hazel catkins – are all out, and everywhere the buds on the trees are swelling and young plants are breaking through the earth into the sunlight. No sunshine today, though, it's a steely grey light and the hills are misty, the air damp.

I reach the copse where the Willows are and step into a different atmosphere. I have a strong sense of community and communication. Do trees communicate with each other? I sense their communication with me, so I have to assume they do. There is an underlying linking energy here – it feels as though each Willow is a part of the others, all united as one Willow family. I imagine their roots below ground, interlinking and touching as they communicate through the dark living Earth.

I stand amongst the Willows and look up into the tangle of their yellow-orange branches – such a bright vibrant colour against the grey sky. I fancy I can hear them singing! It's just the wind in their branches, I know, but the sensation stays with me. I lean against the trunk of one of the Willow trees and let my energy merge with the energy of the tree. I breathe with the tree, slowly and deeply, and feel the sap rising from the roots, surging up the tree in waves of energy. I experience a gentle but strong power that hums with the pulse of the Earth, drawn up by the returning strength of the Sun and the pull of the Full Moon.

It's a cold day, so I need to keep moving, and I have come to clear up the rubbish that always seems to collect here. I've brought plastic bags and rubber gloves and it is soon done. There has been a lot of wind lately and I find there are a lot of twigs and small branches down. I gather these up to take home. I will use the wood for willow wands and talismans, as I prefer to use wood that has naturally been shed by the tree. I thank the trees for their gifts, colour and energy, and set off for home again with the bundle of branches and a bag of rubbish for the bin. I feel changed by my time with the Willows in the little copse. I feel part of the rising energy of the trees and the Earth, and feel that I am connected to Nature and the natural world around me.

When I get home I cut several wands from the Willow branches, one for myself and several for giveaways. As I cut each wand and talisman, I visualize an energetic link to the Willows in the copse, keeping the energy open between the trees and the wands. Willow brings connection to what is within. Coupled with this is its active power, its quickness of growth and communication, which encourages openness and action from the intuition or inspired leaps of the imagination. I poke the thinner twigs into a large pot of wet compost and leave them where they will get the Sun. They should take root and can then be planted back out in the copse or in the garden for quick-growing screens and bowers.

As I carve and sand my Willow wand I realize that Willow energy is much the same energy as Hermes Mercurius and in my mind's eye I give her/m a living Willow wand. S/he is highly delighted with this and I see her/m in my imagination like a Faerie spirit, flitting about with her wand!

I also realize that this has been a good bit of synchronicity, as Willow is just the energy I need to activate open communication with Spirit Guides and Angels.

Angels, Spirit Guides and Guardians

I am beginning to sense that Angels are everywhere and that I have been aware of their presence, the energy and vibration that could be called Angel, for a long time. Previously I have named this 'Presence', 'Guardian' or 'Spirit Guide' and I have experienced it in powerful transformative moments, at powerful places in the landscape, through meditation, trance and daydream. It is a connection to the in-between place, the interface between Spirit and Matter where the two touch and the energy is fluid and potent.

In their long history Angels have not always been depicted in the way that they are now, which has become crystallized during the last few centuries. We probably all have a similar image of Angels as young, beautiful, androgynous, white-skinned creatures, radiating Light and Love, with wings, bare feet and flowing white robes. We also have the little cherub baby Angels, a view of them which completely diminishes their power. These images have been fuelled by artists and religious writings, but they are symbolic images that attempt to give form to a transcendental state, which is why the Angels are depicted with wings. Such images are a long way from the thousands upon tens of thousands of angelic hosts, the mighty abundant communion of Angels, the radiant celestial beings of awesome power and abilities of much earlier writings.

Our view of Angels is once again on the move. Some say we are calling them in as the Earth is in crisis and we are in crisis. As we become free from the doctrines of religion, we are free to make sense of Angels for ourselves. The images we have of Angels could also change at this point as we gain a new impression of this ethereal presence as energy or vibration.

The awareness of non-human spirits is found in all traditions, religions and cultures throughout the world. They are a unifying link that is common to our world family and I'm interested in how they can help us create a common bond and experience of Spirit worldwide.

From what I understand, Angels exist as vibrational energy or Light, outside Time and outside Matter. They seem to be multi-dimensional beings of great power, able to enter and leave the Matrix at will. They may shapeshift, develop form, adjust their frequency and enter our world. Their energy is felt as a Presence and because they originate and exist in the Spirit Realms they are filled with Unconditional or Universal Love. They radiate goodness and goodwill, and they are here to help us.

It is said by those who channel the words of Angels that if we want their help, we have to ask them, as they cannot interfere in our affairs without our asking. The same is said of the Guardians, Spirit Guides or Spirit helpers of the Celtic Pagan tradition. A commonly held belief that links in here is we are each assigned a Guardian Angel or Spirit Guide at birth to be our special helper throughout our life and again we can ask them for help in times of need. I am interested in how we ask for help and who or what we are addressing when we do.

Generally, it is accepted that Angels are intermediaries between the Spirit Realms and humankind. But as Spirit is the connecting Unifying Essence of Life, do we therefore send them to ourselves? Do we create them? Do we personify aspects of our own transcendental energy so that we can work with it? Are they part of our own internal reality, our Otherworld? Are they part of ourselves? Or are we able to communicate with powers beyond us, with benevolent beings that will help us in times of need? Are Angels transcendental entities travelling between realities and dimensions?

I emerge from a daydream, catching a memory of a time when my lack of Love brought me great unhappiness and a blue

Angel figure unexpectedly appeared to me in a meditation vision and laid her hands on my shoulders and loved me even though at the time I couldn't Love myself. I remember how her Love poured into me, wave upon wave, which I felt wash through my body, and how I shuddered with the power of it, and how I cried the much-needed tears of release. The Angel's Love, compassion and healing filled me up and led me out of the state of despair I was in. It was a powerful and transformative moment in my life and I am very grateful for that Angel's visit to me all those years ago. Her presence was so real to me at the time and is even now as I remember the experience. I light a candle for that Angel of Love with gratitude and appreciation of her gift and the transformation it brought to my life.

I light another candle to acknowledge the Sprit Realms all around me, breathing in my connection to other energies around me. I acknowledge the presence of Guardians, Spirit Guides, the Genius Loci (the Spirit of Place), Dryads or Tree Spirits, Daemons, the Faerie Spirits (Faeries also have wings and grant favours), the Gods and Goddesses, the archetypes and the myriad of Spirit beings that fill our myths and legends. These to me are all forms of angelic presence. There is no doubt in my mind that there is a power available to us all, power and energy that exists beyond our normal reality and can be called upon for help and assistance in times of need. The question in my mind is how to call. So I meditate and keep a line open to the Muse Angel and the Timeless Mysteries to send me some inspiration.

I have a lot of questions and very few answers, but I don't feel the need for answers now. There is alchemy here as I unite what I know with what I intuitively sense and I open the channels of communication between myself, Angels and Spirit Guides. I am open to the alchemy, the Union of Spirit and Matter in me. I am open to the possibility that in the Realms of Spirit there are powerful benevolent entities that long to help us and I send out my thoughts and Love and know that on an energetic level they are being received and are circulating back to me.

February 8th
Peace Garden

As a focus for Peace and meditation I begin to create an area in my garden dedicated to Peace, with a place to sit in peaceful meditation and contemplation. I choose a place at the bottom of the garden that gets the evening Sun and I picture myself sitting there enjoying some Peace and contentment at the end of a busy day! I plan to have a bench and a bower, to plant Roses and sweet-smelling herbs.

Before I begin work I light a candle from the Peace Flame and take it out in a candle lantern to my chosen spot. I make a prayer and dedication: 'To inner Peace and to Peace in the world!' Using a stake and a piece of string, I mark out a semi-circle to represent the rainbow, symbol of Unity and hope, and will build the bower and dig the flowerbeds within it.

While I am digging I think about inner Peace and how what is within us is reflected in all we do. Inner Peace creates outer Peace, and world Peace begins with Peace in the heart and Peace of mind. This means raising our awareness of our negative emotions that are fed by our fear and insecurities and uniting them with their opposites, as I learned in the Separation and Union experiences of alchemy. Fear is transformed through trust and greed is transformed by a wish to share. World Peace will grow as we each make the choice to trust each other, to share the world and her resources for the benefit of all Life. It will strengthen as we follow the Love in our hearts and refuse to hate, refuse to kill and refuse to support those who do.

February 20th
At the Dark of the Moon

It is time to create a new shrine area in my room so that I can anchor my new intentions and ideas here. My present shrine was created in the deep stillness of Midwinter, but Imbolc is stirring in me now, the Earth is quickening, the Fertile Force is rising and I am responding to this in many new ways. I decide to hang my big rainbow PEACE flag on the wall behind the shrine. I am inspired by the idea that Peace in the world is linked to Peace in the hearts of the people of the world. I think of all the families who lose their loved ones through war and the children whose childhood is destroyed by war, all the suffering, all the loss and death and destruction of cultures and of communities.

I place the gold candle at the centre of the shrine and light it with the Peace Flame: 'For World Peace, for Peace in the hearts of all people, Peace between nations, Peace between world religions.'

The Imbolc Dark Moon is the right time to plant seeds — actual seeds as well as virtual seeds. Planting now gives a seed time to rest in the Dark, to gather its power. This is natural alchemy. The gradual pull of the Moon as it waxes to Full and the increase in the Light at night will help the seed to grow.

I want to find clarity for the seeds of my new intentions. Which of the many threads that I am exploring do I really want to focus on? I plant some Lavender seeds for the Peace garden and then decide to make an 'Imbolc Maid', a doll traditionally created at Imbolc, and use the creative process to anchor my thoughts. I think of it as an Imbolc Angel or Imbolc Muse and this brings focus to my thoughts on Spirit Guides and Angels.

I begin with one of the Willow sticks, wrapping a strip of material round the top of the stick to make a head and winding pipe cleaners around the stick to make the arms. Then I wrap it all with coloured wool. I tie on strips of net and muslin and sew on sequins and beads and my Imbolc

doll looks very much like an Angel.
Because they are created on a stick,
these dolls can be 'planted' in a plant
pot or stood in a vase amongst some
living twigs.

I bring my Imbolc Angel out and plant
it in the ground where my Peace garden is to
be, as a symbol of my trust in the presence of
Angels and Guardians and their willingness to
help everyone who is sincerely making the journey for inner
and outer Peace.

March 2nd

Imbolc Walk with the Elementals

This is Marion's walk and we agree to walk with
mindfulness, staying in the moment, keeping our awareness
with the Earth and not talking unless it is part of sharing
the magic of the moment, pointing out something we see and
want to share, or sharing a powerful thought.

It's a cold morning with a brilliant blue sky and we
stride out with our breath smoking before us. It's so cold and
completely exhilarating! Blue sky and white frost! So beautiful!
We go over a couple of stiles and then we are in the woods,
standing beside the most glorious huge old Chestnut tree
that Marion calls 'Grandmother Chestnut'.

We admire her, touch her, celebrate her, feel her deep,

calm presence here on the edge of the wood. We've entered her world now, the world of the brown and black woods, here at the winter's end. We are here at this moment of turning, as the Life Force stirs deep within the Earth and we see the first bright green Bluebell leaves showing bravely through the leaf mould. The white trunks of the Silver Birch trees are lit up and shining in the shafts of sunlight. Everything is steaming where the Sun touches, bringing a misty eerie atmosphere! A fairyland! We head off deep into the heart of the woods.

We come to a clearing and stand for a while bathed in sunshine, light and warmth. I feel I could slip out of Time here and give into its pull, feeling the pulse of the land beneath my feet and the presence of the awakening trees all around the edge of the clearing, mostly Crab Apple trees, ancient and gnarled. I slip back from a fleeting glimpse of a daydream and enjoy the faces of my dearest friends, heads turned upwards, bathing in the sunlight, the beauty of this moment reflected in their ecstatic faces. We are all united in this moment, all joined together in a moment of wonder and delight.

We walk on through hidden pathways that only Marion knows and then we come to the 'Threshold Oaks', two Oak trees that stand on either side of the path and create an entrance, a doorway or threshold. Here we stop and wait and meditate on what we will consciously take with us across the threshold. This is our Imbolc moment.

I have been thinking a lot about our world. We stand at the threshold between the old industrial and scientific ages and new possibilites for a sustainable, more caring way forward. There are so many diverse interests and opinions and yet the one thing we need is Unity and the one uniting force that is common to us all is the Love in our hearts. We stand on a threshold that is full of the potential for togetherness, for being one world family, caring for each other, open-hearted, generous and compassionate, sharing this Earth. It is the collective dream of many people all over the world, a vision of a future we can all bring in if enough people believe in it and activate it in their lives right now.

And this is Imbolc, a time in the Earth's cycle for planting seeds and firing up our visions, to aim for the Gold, to reach for the highest dreams. I believe in the power of Universal Love to bring about healing – healing ourselves, healing each other, healing the hurts of nations and healing the Earth. I know the powerful alchemy of its transformative energy and I have to acknowledge it and act on it, to help manifest this dream. So I plant this vision of one united world family and Peace in the world and ask the Spirit Guides, the Angels and the Ancestors to do all they can to help us as I step through the opening between the Threshold Oaks.

We each step through in turn, with ceremony, touching a sacred moment inside ourselves as we make our conscious Imbolc connections.

Marion knows these woods well and has created a mythology of the places she visits regularly. Certain places lend themselves to ceremonies or rituals, or are places to pause and acknowledge their energy or make a symbolic gesture. It brings the landscape alive and opens communion with the Spirit of the land. It helps us to be receptive to a change in the atmosphere, to feel the Spirit of the place, or Spirit moving within us.

We visit the 'Tree That Gave Birth to a Stone', a magical tree whose roots are wrapped round a stone. We stop here for a moment's contemplation of the power of Nature and then wind along pathways, crossing springs and streams that seep out from deep within the Earth. I am mesmerized by the gurgling, chuckling water and am filled with its song and visions of the underground tunnels and passageways that lie under these limestone hills.

At Imbolc springs and wells were once honoured as the powerful interface where the water rose up from the dark earth into the light. Now we find a place where the water is bubbling out from a large mossy stone on the hillside. It is a natural spring which may have once been marked by the stones that now lie around it. There is a special atmosphere here which we all feel and tune in to, standing quietly together, letting the Spirit of Place speak to our hearts. We gather twigs, leaves and stones to create a pattern on the ground by the spring to honour this moment, the Spirit of Water, the Spirit of the woods, the Spirit of Imbolc and our day out together.

HERMES MERCURIUS

Hermes Mercurius is in me now. S/he is shining Light from within me, leading me outwards, with my newfound realizations, my new intentions, hopes and visions for the fertile time ahead. My inner journey with her/m is transformed into the outer journey and I see her/m as a Spirit Guide and Angel who has been with me for a long time, helping me gain insights and understanding, helping me experience the multi-dimensional world in which I belong. S/he brings me an awareness of all the many different ways I have of perceiving and relating to this rich multi-faceted reality we call Life. I balance my conscious logical thinking with a desire to trust my inner world as a valid asset, to follow my intuition if it feels right, to learn from my inner visions and explore the synchronistic messages and events that illuminate the way.

I unite with Hermes Mercurius and let these unfolding understandings take flight within me, drifting between the worlds, resting in Spirit. And then s/he offers me yet another gift: the gift of freedom; the freedom to choose to be part of the whole

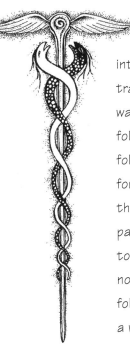

interconnected Web of Life; the freedom to transform myself and my life in whatever way makes sense for me; the freedom to follow my deepest longings and wishes, to follow my visions and dreams and to search for the Unity inside myself, in my life and in the world; the freedom to follow irrational paths, into chaos if needs be; the freedom to follow my heart and Unconditional Love, no matter where it leads; the freedom to follow the magic, my happiness, to act on a whim, to be wild and spontaneous.

I know that true freedom is united with responsibility. I know that all things are connected and everything that I do affects everything else and is reflected back to me as part of the whole interconnected Web of Life. I accept this responsibility with all my words, thoughts and actions. I embrace the freedom, for it is my freedom to grow and to learn from my own experiences. I may make 'mistakes', but alchemy is not about making something right or wrong. When I acknowledge difficulties, I see them as fertile moments, pointing to new ways forward. They are not places to stay stuck in, but points of departure. They hold the key to new solutions

and create a doorway to the next level of awareness. Alchemy includes all things as part of the whole, as part of a cycle or process, so that through my experiences I learn to develop true integrity and true spirituality.

I accept my responsibility to freedom, wherever it may lead me, for it also includes the freedom to backtrack, to say 'I'm sorry', to try again with new understanding. I am open to freedom as part of my journey, for in freedom lies the gift of choice, courage, trust and Love. I unite them all together as I step through the doorway into the next part of the cycle, with gratitude for Hermes Mercurius, Spirit Guide and Angel, and for the Light of inspiration s/he brings.

The Spirit of Hermes Mercurius comes with me, filling me with the magic of alchemy and delightful zest for Life. For this is the fertile time and all Life is on the move. Life is ready to manifest itself and I am ready to experience the new unfolding journey. I am free to flow and become my heart's desire, to bring my deepest wishes from the Spirit Realms into the realms of manifestation.

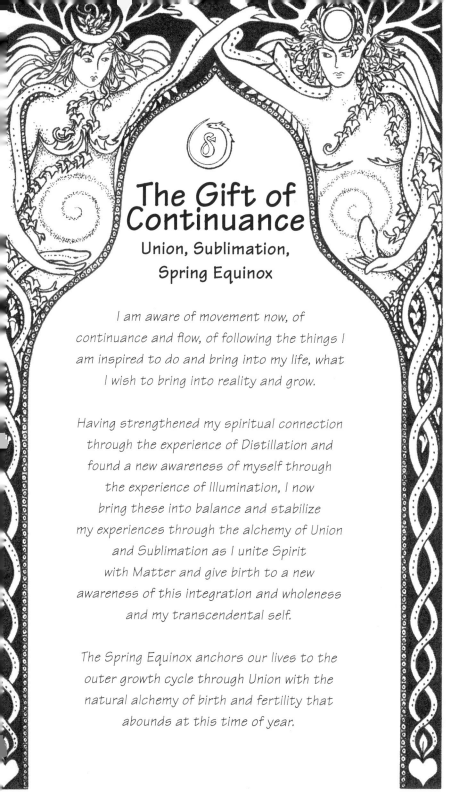

The Gift of Continuance

Union, Sublimation, Spring Equinox

I am aware of movement now, of continuance and flow, of following the things I am inspired to do and bring into my life, what I wish to bring into reality and grow.

Having strengthened my spiritual connection through the experience of Distillation and found a new awareness of myself through the experience of Illumination, I now bring these into balance and stabilize my experiences through the alchemy of Union and Sublimation as I unite Spirit with Matter and give birth to a new awareness of this integration and wholeness and my transcendental self.

The Spring Equinox anchors our lives to the outer growth cycle through Union with the natural alchemy of birth and fertility that abounds at this time of year.

The Alchemical Experience of Union

In alchemy, Union is viewed through the metaphor of the Chymical Wedding. Here at the second Union of the cycle, Sol and Luna are elevated to King and Queen and out of their Union comes a royal birth. Through this we are encouraged to seek our royal nature so that we don't fall prey to the distortion of diminishment and underestimate the vastness of our spiritual selves and our abilities. This experience is the elevation of our spiritual selves, the completion of our whole selves.

Union is an experience of the Unity and Oneness in all things and is only possible through surrender of the Self. It is not to be confused with an elevation of the ego.

The dynamic energy of Union is fusion. Whatever is united is fused together to create a new energy.

Creating this fusion is another skill that I improve the more I practise it. It is similar to what I have been doing with trees for years. I call it 'settling my energy in with theirs'. I wasn't taught to do this, it just feels like a natural thing to do as I merge my energy with the energy of the tree and become one with the tree. The tree is already One with the Web of Life and I realign my own energy with its help. In this new state of Oneness I briefly become transfigured and step between the worlds. I reach another level of awareness and give birth to a new part of myself.

By surrendering myself to the experience of merging, I am able to become One with anything – with the land, a mountain, a tree, the past, the future, the present, a Spirit Guide or Angel. The possibilities are endless. This is alchemy and transfiguration and it is happening inside me, creating a new transcendental experience.

The key to transcendence lies in my ability to surrender my Self to the Union. Transcendence can also be reached through other forms of surrender, through surrendering to Universal Love, which facilitates a natural expansion into the Limitless Infinite energy of Spirit and the transcendental self.

Tantra

Tantra is a spiritual practice of Hinduism and Buddhism and is a path of spirituality through Unity that includes sacred sexuality as part of its teaching. Alchemy, Paganism and Tantra have been labelled scandalous and heretical for their validation of sexuality as a transformative spiritual experience. But when physical Union fuses with Unconditional Love and total surrender, a state of Bliss is created that expands our senses, our minds, our hearts and our perceptions and brings a natural transcendental experience. Lovemaking becomes a form of meditation as Spiritual Union becomes the desire, not sexual gratification. Sacred sexuality is the slowing down to a place of feeling and 'presence', where Time melts and becomes Eternity and we are 'making' Love with Love.

The aim of Tantric sexuality is towards continuity rather than conclusion, towards creating a lasting experience of loving Bliss rather than a quick orgasm. Bliss is a heightened state, an experience of Universal Love, full of well-being and healing. Tantric sexuality is like the Distillation and Illumination experiences in alchemy. The Divine loving energy is circulating, ascending and descending in continuous cycles. It opens us to the experience of transcendence, an experience of Oneness that is felt in each and every one of our cells and touches the realms of the Angels and Spirit Guides. Through this experience we are transfigured into a new state of transcendental Love, true ecstasy, creating a shift in perception, a shift outside Time and Space, expanding in all directions, inside and out. We merge with the Essence and experience limitless energy. We can bathe in it, become One with it, share it between us and also consciously send it out, harness it as a usable force, picturing it softening hearts and filling them with Love, bringing Peace into the world.

Sacred sexual Union was seen as a short cut to spiritual ecstasy because it was not lasting. However, I believe that when we have experienced something once we can find it again and re-experience it in our imagination and inner world. The energy continues to exist inside us and we can strengthen it from here, tapping into it whenever its energy is needed.

Any experience of Unity can be recalled and used in this

way as a focus for personal healing, to heal all separations and can be sent out as a force for transformation and change in the world.

The Alchemical Experience of Sublimation

The alchemical experience of Sublimation grows out of Union, giving birth to a new part of ourselves, an experience of the Divine or Spirit that is an inclusive part of our whole selves.

Chemically, Sublimation is similar to Distillation. It is the changing of a solid to a vapour and then back again. Alchemically, it is our growing awareness of our ability to sublimate, to pass energetically between Matter and Spirit and to experience the sublime, our Divine nature inside ourselves. From the Latin sub, meaning 'below' and limen, meaning 'threshold', this is our ability to experience the 'Threshold', the potent place 'between the worlds'. Here the alchemist becomes transfigured by the pure energy of Love and Unity, becoming a healer, and Light-worker, able to transcend Time and place.

Sublimation is related to our ability to transfer and to direct psychic energy for healing and service. From this new state of being come new desires, new ways forward. In alchemy, this is called the birth of the royal child. New Life grows from the experience of Sublimation, with the manifestation of new desires.

I experience Sublimation as Unconditional Love that gives all and asks for nothing, that comes from a place that is pure in heart and in Essence. This is a powerful place inside me that feels potent, alive and naturally vibrant, pure, Lifebecoming and Life-awakening. It is a place where I feel light and loose, mutable, and fluid. I am able to relax here, float in the flow and Unity of Life.

I am filled with a desire to share, to give, to help others and humanity. This desire is without ulterior motive. I give without needing or wanting thanks or reward. I give to be of service, to help others and the Earth, simply this. This is Spirit in action, spreading benevolence to increase benevolent energy in the world.

I create it for myself in the first place, seeking out this united place inside myself. Once I find it, I am able to connect to it again. The alchemy happens first inside me and through the experience of Sublimation I am able to circulate inner Peace and Unity outwards from my centre, beginning with myself and then moving to my family, spreading outwards to my friends and extended family and out into the world. This also returns to me, bringing an increase of inner Peace, Unity and Love energy to my life. I become filled by it and therefore my giving is from a place that is full, that does not lack anything. I give because it is a natural part of the flow, it is the only way to go, a natural continuance. I am all joined up – giving and receiving are One.

There is always the possibility of a twist in the tail of the Ouroboros that breaks the flow of Universal Love and

Unity. This is the human element, the turning away from the flow of Unity through the need to feed the ego. The alchemy of Sublimation is not present in those who give to gain something for themselves, so I consciously check that I am giving from a place of Unconditional Love, giving without attachment, without a need to get something in return, and I am not giving to appease guilt, to self-gratify or to coerce, to create obligation or subservience.

Sublimation is new Life that grows from a true fusion of Spirit and Matter. It is a continuance of the essential Unity of Life, the Essence, and is the essential energy of the Philosopher's Stone, the Gold and the Elixir of Life. These are all gifts of continuance, things that continue and grow from this new awareness of integration and wholeness. This is the Gold that increases, the Philosopher's Stone that anchors Spirit in my consciousness and creates transformation through my every action. It is healing energy that can be sent out to increase Peace and harmony in the world.

The Alchemy of the Spring Equinox

The Spring Equinox is the first day of spring, celebrated on March 20th–23rd in the Northern Hemisphere and September 20th–23rd in the Southern Hemisphere (see chart on page 27). This is a celebration of balance and Union between the Light and the Dark cycles of the year, between the Sun and the Moon, between Yang and Yin, Fire and Water. From this dynamic joining of opposites come new Life, transformation and manifestation.

From here to Midsummer Solstice, the days will lengthen as the Sun returns, bringing increasing strength and warmth, and the nights will shorten. This is the beginning of the growing period, the season of manifestation. It is a time for unions of all kinds, for fertility and birth. Out of Union comes new Life. This is the natural alchemy of Union inherent in all Life on Earth at this time.

Here at the Spring Equinox, the alchemy lies in the transference of energy from the inside to the outside, from Spirit into Matter. What is within is flowing towards manifestation. Across the wheel at the Autumn Equinox (see page 93) the alchemy lies in the transference of energy from Matter into Spirit, taking the essence of what we have manifested back inside for assimilation and understanding. This delightful balance of our inner and outer worlds flows through our lives as each Equinox helps us to be aware of the natural movement and direction of the cycle.

In the Celtic tradition, the Goddess of fertility is celebrated at the Spring Equinox. She has many names but is most commonly known as Eostre or Oestre. This is the root of the word oestrus, the time in the reproduction cycle when the female produces oestrogen, the hormone that stimulates ovulation. The Church overlaid this festival with Easter, with its theme of the continuance of Life.

Oestre is the Spring Maiden and the Celtic Pagan traditions celebrate her sexual Union with the ardent young male, the Green Man, the Spirit of new growth, for without his seed there would be no fertility. Their cosmic Union ensures the fertility of the land is re-energized through all sexual acts, especially at this time of the year. Sexuality is part of our natural cycle and a natural expression of attraction between two people. It is a vibrant expression of the Life Force, and of new Life that follows Union, the potential within the egg and the creative place of new beginnings.

The alchemy of the Spring Equinox represents the joining of opposite forces to create a blending of energy which is alive, potent and expansive. I use this time for balance, and for bringing together what I wish to unite. Whatever I bring to my thoughts will grow – my Love, my wishes, my intentions, my visions, my hopes and dreams. Whatever I give my energy to will grow, so I consciously give Life to the seeds I have been nurturing through the winter and early spring.

I am aware of movement from within to without, aware of the energy surge that propels Life forward into the new growth cycle and I hold on to my links to the Spirit Realms. I consciously unite my spiritual journey with my daily life as I move forward into the expansive growth cycle, so that I bring Spirit to the Fertile Force of manifestation.

The Joining of the Above and the Below

The alchemical Union of Spirit and Matter is a universal experience open to us all, an intrinsic part of ourselves, a place within, a place of being. We are all able to unite with Spirit. As an alchemist, I experience it as the Ouroboros, as an internal feeling of being 'all joined up'. There is no separation between Spirit and Matter. They are the same thing. We are whole and complete when we envision it so.

'As Above, so Below' is the alchemical maxim that represents our ability to transmute into a transcendent state. From this experience of Oneness come both personal transformation and the ability to transmute Matter. This is essentially what happens in spiritual healing and I am open to expanding this further. It is linked to the experience of Sublimation, the experience of the Unity of Life and the natural flow of continuance.

Alchemy uses symbols and metaphors to facilitate a transcendent state in the mind. To understand a symbol, the conscious and unconscious minds are joined together, and this creates a shift in perception and a breakthrough into a new understanding. This new perception exists in the transcendent function of the mind until it is earthed in actual experience and then it transfers into consciousness.

Transcendence is a natural ability, a natural evolution of the psyche or Soul. The symbol-forming function of the psyche has been called the 'Higher Self' or 'Holy Guardian

Angel'. These titles interest me, as they refer to that part of myself that connects me to the 'Inner Guide' and to our natural ability to receive guidance from beyond our rational mind, 'to step between the worlds'.

I am conscious of receiving messages and guidance from beyond myself through the serendipitous coincidences and synchronicities that I often experience. These are the signs and omens our ancestors would have followed and I keep an open mind to them. When they happen I feel I am somehow in the right place at the right time – another experience of being 'all joined up'.

I am increasingly aware of the flow and movement between Spirit and Matter. I am all I am longing for, all I yearn for and desire. What I yearn for is what I manifest. I have free will and I have choice.

My desires are the catalyst for the reality I create for myself. All is connected. All is Unity in the flow between Spirit and Matter. All is One.

We are the interconnected Web of Life. We are all making the circuits for the energy to flow along, and ultimately there is no Above and no Below, only the whole.

March 8th

International Womens Day

I am aware of the transition in the Earth's energy and my energy at this time. I ask myself, 'What do I wish to consciously unite at the Spring Equinox? What do I wish to grow more of in my life and in the world? What do I want to encourage, to give my attention to, so that it has the best possible chance of manifestation?'

I feel the stirrings of my seed intentions. I see new directions, new possibilities and ways of bringing these seeds into reality. I use this moment to make heartfelt connections that help me to stay focused on what I choose to grow, what I choose to be open to manifesting in my life.

I light my gold candle with the Love Fire and one by one merge with my seeds and new intentions.

I affirm my choice to stay connected and open to the Spirit Realms and my understanding of them so far. I am also open to creating change through my interaction with the subtle energy of Life.

I affirm my quest for inner and outer Peace and I picture healing energy flowing around the world, picture people at Peace with themselves so that they no longer feel the need to make war on others. I picture all people respecting the Earth and the sacred Elements of Life.

I affirm my wish to work with others, especially women, to bring Peace and Love into the world. I picture the energy of goodwill and kindness being passed on between people of all generations, cultures and religions. I see the future as part of the present, and in this present moment we become united as one world family. I unite with a world in which each individual and each culture is able to flourish, where caring and sharing are nurtured and encouraged, where everyone is aware of their part in sustaining and nurturing the whole. I affirm that WE are the active force for change in the world.

I breathe in Spirit and Matter joined as One. I breathe in Universal Love as a catalyst for change and healing, I breathe in joy and happiness, so that I see my seeds growing with this joy and happiness in their roots as they continue into Life.

March 13th

Visit to the Spring

I have a strong urge to head off to the spring that I visited last at Lammas. I plan a day for myself, a vision quest day of contemplation and meditation, a day for the Spirit of the Muse, for being with the rising energy of the Earth and feeling this rising energy in me.

I want to focus on how I can balance my inner world with my outer world in practical ways, how I can keep the communication channels open between what I am feeling and sensing on the inside and my everyday life. I feel a need to prepare now for the next part of the cycle. I can feel the shift in the Earth's energy. It's tugging at me to move and I want to use it wisely.

When I get to the river, the waters are high and have a kind of insistent power of quickening Life and purpose. The

stepping stones are tumbled out of line and I can't get across
and have to walk up the river to find a new crossingplace.
It's so good to be up here in these hills again, the clouds
racing across the sky, flashes of sunshine lighting up the
trees. Everywhere I look I see the return of new growth – buds
bursting, leaves unfurling, each tree surrounded by a haze of
pink, red and green opening buds.

I feel quite hare-like and exhilarated by it all and run
along the pathways in the woods, jumping on and off rocks,
enjoying a sense of freedom and of joy of Life. I feel I am
part of Nature, part of the awakening energy! As I near
the spring I sense the energy change and soften and I slow
down and slip into a state of receptivity, of meditative
stillness and alertness.

And there it is, the same 'Presence' that I always
feel here! I have always identified it as the 'Guardian'
of the spring and have always felt deeply humbled by
the power I feel here. As I step into the energy I sense a
welcome and feel the strange sensation of the very place
smiling at me! Because I feel so welcomed, I step into the
Presence of the Guardian. I can't describe it any other
way. I experience a merging, a Union with the place I have
never experienced before. I now sense that what I perceived
as the 'Guardian' of the spring doesn't just protect the
spring but IS the spring!

I experience Oneness with the spring, Oneness with the
land and with the Spirit of Water that flows out from deep

inside the Earth. I experience a detachment from my body, which remains sitting on a rock watching the water pour out of the spring, and merge with the Spirit of the spring. I am the laughing, bubbling Spirit of Water, released from the depths of the Earth, out in the light and the Sun. I am sparkling Fire, reflecting light. I am the Spirit of freedom and adventure, racing off down the stream, over rocks, feeding the land. I am the flow of fertile abundant Life!

From this altered state, I am also able to merge with the land around me and I become the deep silent stillness of the trees around the spring. For this brief moment I experience myself as transient energy. Time and Matter are illusions and I slip through the Web of Light and Spirit.

After a while the experience fades and I am back in my normal reality again, sitting on the rock by the gushing water of the spring. I collect spring water and thank the Spirit of the spring in a new way, by sending my energy stream out once again to touch the Presence of this place with Love and Gratitude, with my heart open and smiling. This experience of Union is part of me now, it is inside me, I can feel it, touch it and contact it again. It continues! I head back along the path, taking this understanding of Union and continuance with me.

When I get home I need to ground my experience, so I write about it in my journal. I have experienced these shifts in consciousness before, these moments of Unity when I have become one with a tree, or with the Spirit of a place, but never as deeply as this. I am able to make sense of it through my work with alchemy. I am aware that I have experienced a shift in my understanding of Union and from this experience I have given birth to a new part of myself, a new level of awareness that has Life within me and continues on.

March 23rd

Spring Equinox with the Elementals

We meet together to celebrate the Spring Equinox and we have brought things that reflect this: spring flowers, small chocolate eggs and egg-shaped stones to decorate. We use these to create an Equinox shrine, lighting lots of candles and creating a beautiful focus. We gather in a circle around our shrine and sing each of the Five Elements into our circle and into our hearts. We welcome our Spirit Guides, our Ancestors and our Descendants, the Spirit of Oestre and the Spirits of Hearth and Home.

It becomes clear from the check-in that we have all been very busy and are all exhausted and feel our energy is depleted. We decide to focus on what we need to give ourselves to have more energy.

We each take an egg stone and focus on new directions and new beginnings as we decorate our stone with coloured crayons. After this we decide to make a big pile of cushions in the middle of the room and we take it in turns to lie on the cushions and receive healing. We all work intuitively together. We tone notes, massage feet, head and hands, chant, stroke, speak intuitively and channel healing energy. It is very powerful and uplifting, releasing and energizing both

in the giving and the receiving. We are all filled up with Love again. It creates a bond between us, both through the uniting of our energies and through the Love and healing that were given and received.

We celebrate our insights for new directions with each chocolate egg we eat and we pass round spring water. We then close our circle by singing our gratitude to the Spirits of Hearth and Home, the Spirit of Oestre, the Ancestors and Descendants, our Spirit Guides and Angels, and to Spirit, to Earth, to Water, to Fire and to Air. 'We take them into our hearts and out into the world.'

March 27th
The Alchemy of the Five Elements

My experience at the spring has affected me profoundly and I am compelled to continue and grow with the new understanding that I experienced there.

I feel still and peaceful this morning and I meditate for a long time, feeling deeply connected to Spirit within myself. I seem to have found a new skill of merging and uniting with whatever I put my imagination to and I can apply this to many things. I welcome the energy of each of the Five Elements in this new way, merging with the Spirit of the element and wrapping them all around me in a circle of linked energy.

I know I am always part of the whole all the time and that the Elements are united in me. In this way I become each Element.

I am the Spirit of Air. I am the Spirit of communication and of initiation. I am in all new beginnings, in all new seeds that grow. I am in the springtime as the new growth cycle begins. I am in the words that are spoken and the thoughts that are open. I am Spirit of change, blowing away old concepts, old limitations and old ideas, making way for new understanding, new perceptions and new shifts in awareness. I am my conscious breath. I am my conscious communication, speaking truth and seeking Unity, initiating positive and healthy new beginnings.

I am the Spirit of Fire, bringing passion and inspiration to new beginnings! I am spontaneity and the freedom to run wild, to celebrate expansion and self-expression. I am laughter and joy. I am the warmth of the Sun and the active growth cycle. I am action, the generosity of giving. I am active energy seeking Unity. I unite my outer Fire with my inner Sacred Fire to bring transformation from within to inspired actions out in the world.

I am the Spirit of Water, the fluidity and quickening of Life. I am the flowing power of the spiral, the vortex, the self-cleansing energy of movement. I am the Spirit and Life of healing that flows and seeks equilibrium. I am the rain that swells the new seeds so that they grow. I am the fertility of reflection. I am the power of the heart, the fuel of Love that creates freedom of movement through loving actions and through release of the emotions. I am receptivity and intuition seeking Unity, so that all things find balance and equilibrium.

I am the Spirit of Earth, awakening energy of the land. I am the stabilizing force, bringing new Life from Union. I am the potent force, the Fertile Force and the creation force seeking Unity. I am alive, the living Spirit of Gaia, and I bring transformation and change, death and rebirth in continuous cycles. I am the Spirit of regeneration and I am the continuous Spirit of new Life and growth.

I am Spirit in all things, the interconnected Web of Life. I am Unconditional Love and Light, the spark of Life and creation, the Source of Life. I am Limitless, Infinite, Eternal, the Omnipresent, Quintessence. I am Unity. I am Within and Without. I am the circle, open and yet unbroken, encompassing the All and the Nothing. I am.

The Fertile Force of Healing

Everyone is a healer. We are all capable of transmuting illness, whether it is our own, other people's or the Earth's. Miracles do happen. I keep open to this truth every time I send healing Unity and Love and receive healing Unity and Love.

Universal or Unconditional Love brings transformation through Unity and Oneness, through the creation of a common bond, through the sharing of the energy we all have in common. Love is a power and a catalyst that creates new Life through the experience of giving or receiving of Love. And what has been changed through Love continues and grows through the Fertile Force of Life, Unity and expansion.

Healing and illness are part of the same thing. Illness is energy that is disconnected from Unity and has become stuck. All things are connected and our physical, emotional, mental and spiritual selves contribute to any illness and therefore all contribute to the healing. Like a magnet our consciousness draws towards us what we truly believe. Ideas attract, as do strong convictions or beliefs and strong intentions. We attract illness and we attract healing. Releasing our trapped and buried emotions breathes Life into the healing process, creates movement, flow and the freedom to find equilibrium again. From this comes new Life, the gift of continuance.

Illness can be transmuted. Healing can be instant. I have experienced this miracle and know that it is possible. Healing begins when all separations dissolve, bringing a reconnection to the Oneness of Life. Positive thoughts open our psyches to healing. Body, mind and Soul are connected by imagination, and imagery can alter the intelligence of our cells. Either subconsciously or consciously, we are always in communication with every part of ourselves and every cell responds to the messages we are sending every day. From this perspective we are our own Fertile Force for healing; we are our own healers.

Imagination has been related to the Soul and now I catch a glimpse of this understanding. If I can imagine it, I can experience it. It exists. The Soul has no physical existence except in my imagination and yet I experience it as a place within, a place connected to my heart. Once again I am aware of my imagination as a powerful part of myself, not to be ignored but celebrated and developed as an active metaphysical tool.

Once I have experienced Oneness, I can experience it again through my imagination. I can recall it and reunite with it. It continues to exist inside and outside Time, in my imagination, the transcendent function of the mind. I learn to find this place of Oneness within myself and call it up from the experiences I have had of it and from here it has Life and continues.

If I envision healing as happening in the future, that is where it will always stay, in the future. I step outside Time and focus on what is already mine, I step into certainty and know the healing has already happened. The future begins now in this moment.

HERMES MERCURIUS

Hermes Mercurius has been connected to each unfolding part of my journey. The more I have consciously made the connection, the stronger it has become. At first I was inspired by the energy s/he represented. Gradually, I have assimilated this within myself and now I experience it as part of myself, reflecting my own potential and the potential within us all.

I am at One with the whole and now I move between the worlds like Hermes Mercurius. Through my imagination I am able to travel the inner dimensions, materialise and dematerialise in virtual space at will. I have the choice and I have the freedom.

Life reflects back to me whatever I reflect into it. We are the same Unity. There is no 'there' to go to, there is only here. There is no end, only continuance. I am creating my future now within my present. Whatever I bring to Life or to death continues and is created through the Fertile Force that is limitless and unbound, Infinite and multi-dimensional. I am the Matrix of all possibilities and I am what I believe.

I am Hermes Mercurius, Spirit Guide and Angel, messenger from Spirit, traveller between the worlds.
I am the Spirit of freedom, the Spirit of potential, the Fertile Force that unites Spirit in all things.
I am the bridge-builder bringing Spirit and Matter together as One.
I am inclusive and whole, and I am in you, as you are in me.

We are the flow, the giving and the receiving and we are the Spirit of Continuance, for all Life is expanding circulating energy.
We are the Spirit of our own healing and the source of our own answers.
We have everything we need, right now, here within us.

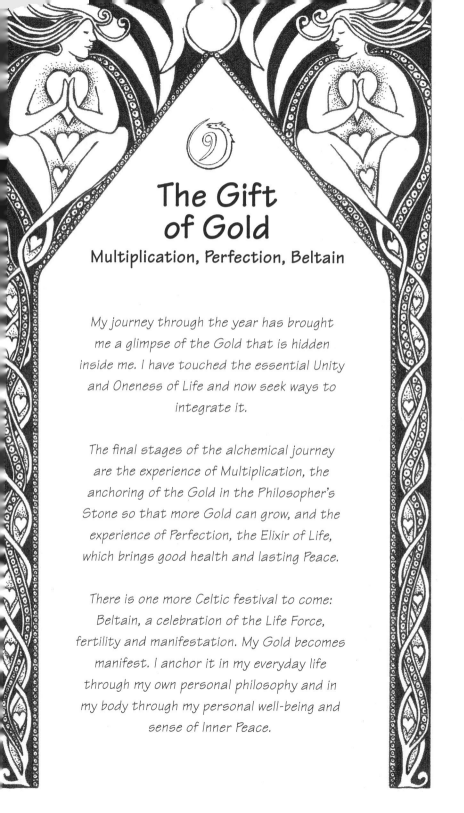

The Gift of Gold

Multiplication, Perfection, Beltain

My journey through the year has brought me a glimpse of the Gold that is hidden inside me. I have touched the essential Unity and Oneness of Life and now seek ways to integrate it.

The final stages of the alchemical journey are the experience of Multiplication, the anchoring of the Gold in the Philosopher's Stone so that more Gold can grow, and the experience of Perfection, the Elixir of Life, which brings good health and lasting Peace.

There is one more Celtic festival to come: Beltain, a celebration of the Life Force, fertility and manifestation. My Gold becomes manifest. I anchor it in my everyday life through my own personal philosophy and in my body through my personal well-being and sense of Inner Peace.

The Alchemical Experience of Multiplication

Common to all mystical traditions is the belief that the multiplicity of the world comes from One Source in which all things are unified. Spirit becomes anchored in Matter, anchored in the present moment, the first unit of Time, and from here it multiplies with whatever it is united with. Creation is the natural energy of the Earth. This final stage of our journey is the realization that what we manifest in life is our choice. To become an alchemist is to consciously engage in creating our own destiny.

This final stage of the alchemical experience looks at the natural laws of manifestation so that we learn to multiply the Gold. To glimpse the Gold once is to find it again.

Throughout alchemical texts we are told that we are the Gold, that it is inside us. We are the quintessential Unity of the Life Force. We are the Oneness. We are the essential energy of Life. There is no separation at the level of energy.

All Life is responding to its own essential energy and whatever is brought to this essential energy multiplies and manifests. The more I strengthen my realization of this, the more I strengthen my connection to the Life Force. For everything multiplies and everything changes with every connection I make, whether it is through my thoughts, my words or my actions. Whatever I give attention to will grow.

The Philosopher's Stone

My Philosopher's Stone is the realization that the Gold I have found lives on in me and creates more Gold with whatever it is united with. Whatever we add to Life – our beliefs, our thoughts, our feelings or our actions – the natural expansion of growth and creation on Earth brings manifestation. Once the Gold is found, it multiplies. This is the natural law of continuation and expansion, the natural energy and flow of manifestation that creates abundance on Earth.

The Philosopher's Stone helps me to anchor these new experiences and insights, so that the Gold becomes 'earthed', stabilized within me and stabilized on the Earth.

I connect to the Gold through daily meditation, which helps me to still my busy mind through focusing on one unit, one thing, such as the breath, a single image, a sound, a word or simple mantra. From this I am able to slip out of Time into an experience of no-thing, Timelessness. This opens me to an experience of the Oneness of Spirit, the Eternal Present, the Limitless Unconditional Essence of Life, and when I surrender myself to it I am filled up with it.

My mercurial nature is able to facilitate a quick connection to this Gold within me whenever I need it. I discover that I can connect to the experience in an instant. I recall how it feels to be there and I am there! I reconnect to it often while I am doing other things, developing a state of mindfulness and Peace within myself. I connect to it quickly in moments of stress and chaos, whenever I am thrown off from my centre. I practise the art of recognizing when I have become disconnected and separated from Unity and Love and reconnect as quickly as possible. I see these moments as lessons to learn from, opportunities for healing and for Love. Acts of Love and kindness, generosity and appreciation all strengthen my connection to the Gold. I look for the things that bring me lasting happiness and strengthen these, so they are what I multiply.

The Alchemical Experience of Perfection

What is Within is reflected Without. The finding of the Gold within has lasting repercussions as it shines out from within us and is reflected in our feelings and our thoughts and all we manifest. This has a profound effect on our essential Life Force and this shift in perception creates internal happiness and Peace, and so we are the source of our own health and well-being.

This final stage in my alchemical journey is a glimpse of Perfection. Once glimpsed, this too can be found again and strengthened. So I practise the 'Art of Being' and I become One with the Unity of Life, the Eternal Present, the flow of Infinite Universal energy. I surrender myself to it and experience being filled with it. I experience the Oneness as Unconditional Energy. When I connect to it I experience joy and Love at my re-Union with the Web of Life. And this is reflected back to me as the Unconditional Love and Joy that I am united with.

This is my Perfection experience. I am the Love that I create. I am the Essence of Life, I am the Oneness, I am the Unity, and I am the flow of my own Life Force. I am my own experience of Perfection and it fills me up with Unconditional Love. It's perfect!

The Elixir of Life

The Elixir of Life is another aspect of the alchemist's Gold. This time it is a liquid, connected to the element of Water, the Flow, the Receptive Force, reflecting harmony from within. We are told that the Elixir is the bringer of good health, long life and immortality, and that it is within us and available to us all. It is carried by the eternal flow of the unseen Life Force and manifests as good health and well-being.

The Elixir is connected to heightened spiritual experiences or mystic experiences and may be a secretion produced by the pineal gland right at the centre of our brains. Ancient civilizations, tribal nations, the religions of the world, philosophers, scientists and mystics all refer to it. It is linked to an experience of the Divine, the Universal Flow of Life and the magical alchemy of the Life Force. It is referred to as a golden liquid, Nectar, the sacred juice, the luminous Distillation of

Heaven. It is known as a healing balm, a Life-giving moisture, a cleansing spiritual dew. The Hindus call it Amrita. To the ancient Greeks it was the Nectar of the Gods or Ambrosia of the Gods that bestowed immortality. It is also known as Chi, the Life Force, Prana, Universal Energy, Universal Love, Mana, Orgone, Psi and Grace.

I experience the Elixir as my receptivity to the Gold within me. I touch it through meditation and the art of being, when I experience the Flow of Life as a continuous circuit of giving and receiving and when I add Love, joy, appreciation, Unity and healing to the Flow. Then I am filled with the Elixir and my cup runs over. I give from a place of fullness and spiritual replenishment and a natural spontaneous altruism. In this way I feel young at heart, liberated, lifted, filled with happiness that shines from within. My spirit is released from the confines of Time and I touch my immortal self... Sometimes!

The Alchemy of Beltain

In the Northern Hemisphere Beltain is celebrated any time around the end of April/beginning of May, especially when the Moon is waxing to Full and the Sun is shining. In the Southern Hemisphere Beltain is celebrated at the end of October/beginning of November. This is the Celtic festival that celebrates outer growth, fertility, new Life and the essential energy of manifestation and creation. It is the final stage of the active Yang cycle of the Sun before it reaches its fullness at the Midsummer Solstice. All of Life is manifesting now as the rampant growth period and the summer fully begin. Beltain is a celebration of the Life Force, of the abundant fertility of the Earth and of ourselves.

Across the circle of the Wheel of the Year (see chart on page 27) is Samhain, also the festival before the Solstice, but this time at the heart of winter. Beltain and Samhain are linked in the Celtic Pagan tradition as times when the veil between the worlds is thin, especially at dawn and dusk. Both are times of transition, energetic interfaces, 'in-between' times.

Samhain is understood as a time to enter the Dark, the Otherworld inside us, a time to contact the Ancestors, Spirit Guides and Guardians. Beltain is traditionally a time to enter the Light, to contact the Otherworld around us, the world of Earth Spirits, Nature Spirits, the world of Faerie and the Dragon Force or Serpent Force of the awakened Earth energies. The Life Force is so strong now it is manifesting other inter-dimensional possibilities. The Earth Dragon, Ley lines or Spirit paths are active now and these lead us to sacred places in the land that enhance our ability to enter other realities.

Beltain is the time for exploring the Web, the Matrix, to enter the interface between Spirit and Matter, to enter the multi-dimensional realms of all possibilities.

This is the fertile time when manifestation is at its peak, traditionally a time to commune with Tree Spirits, to enter the Realms of Faerie and explore the Mysteries that manifest on the edge of our reality such as the little people, the fair folk. Something happens at this time that is unique in the year's cycle, something that echoes back through Time and is still in evidence today through the UFO sightings and crop circle phenomena of the summer months.

Traditionally, people would stay up all night on the eve of Beltain, especially by springs and wells, and would walk the labyrinths and slip into altered states. Beltain is a time for magic, for jumping the Beltain fires to invoke what we want for ourselves now that the Fertile Force is strong. It is the time to reach for our wildest and most expansive visions and dreams. To dare! To manifest!

At Beltain I take chances. I jump through Fire, fire up my vision of what I truly want to manifest in Life. I remember that holding back is a symptom of fear and doubt and all fear is an opportunity for transformation. To block the flow is to block the Life Force and illness results. Illness can be seen as a wake-up call to jump back into Life, to get the flow moving again. As long as I jump into Life I am part of Life, part of the flow, part of the Life Force, and there will always be new experiences to propel me forward and create new insights, new understanding and healing.

I test and strengthen my Gold through my spontaneous actions. Whatever I give my attention to brings manifestation and leads the way to my abundance, the flowering and harvest of all I have created.

Flowing with Fire

The early alchemists believed that the connecting link between Spirit and Matter was the Emanation (from the Latin *menare*, meaning 'to flow') – flowing energy in endless streams, everything connected to everything else, the interconnected Web of Life.

To the alchemist, the energy of creation is the abundant flow of Union, the eternal fertile Life Force that merges and unites with whatever it meets, creating new Life with every part of itself forever. What I bring into Life will grow. What I give my energy and my power to will increase.

At Beltain the element of Fire is coming up to its height. This is Yang Fire, outer Fire that activates the energy of the Fertile Force and creates fertility on Earth. I explore my connection with Fire and what I am activating and setting in motion. I unite Fire with Spirit and feel the powerful energy of the Life Force expanding in all directions simultaneously. Fire is Light. Light is Energy. Fire is Star-Fire, our link to the beginning of Life, Life Fire, Life Force.

Fire is the Spark of Life, the Initiator, the Transformer, the Spirit of Change. What I choose to initiate will continue. What I give to my Spirit Fire will expand outwards, will manifest. My choice to set Life in motion and my will to begin co-create abundance through the transference of energy from 'Within' to 'Without'. Fire is in my intention and what I consciously focus on. Whatever I give attention to and what I concentrate on will grow and will continue. I fire up my passion for the transformative power of Unconditional Love, for this, above all else, is what I want to multiply.

April 23rd
Earth Day

Today is Earth Day and it's one of those perfect spring days. I drop everything else and simply soak up the wonderful fertility of Life. I spend much of my day in the garden, turning over the soil and digging up Dandelions. I wash and dry the roots and lay them out on wicker trays to dry out. I will use these to make root 'coffee'. Many of our wild native plants are edible and I harvest many of these 'weeds' to eat or to dry for winter use. I have introduced many native plants into my garden that can be used in the kitchen or for medicine and it gives me great pleasure at this time of the year to pick their young leaves for salad. They are far better than anything I could buy. I eat them straightaway and they are bursting with the Life Force, the Spirit of the springtime and the Sprit of the land! I also have the wonderful experience of engaging with the natural world around me and I realize that my appreciation, Love and gratitude for the Earth begin in my heart, here in my garden with these plants I grow and harvest.

I plant lots of seeds today, vegetables mostly, directly into the freshly dug beds. As I plant the seeds I send my Love and good wishes with them and plant my ideas and intentions to work with natural alchemy for the good of the Earth.

My Peace garden is taking shape slowly and I'm happy to let it evolve and grow with me. I sit here on the Earth in the sunshine and soak up the peacefulness that I already feel is part of this corner of the garden. I breathe in my commitment to the Earth and hold in my mind's eye that beautiful photo of the Earth from space. I try to simply be with the Earth without blame or judgement about what is wrong. I fire up my most loving and most positive thoughts so that I consciously set in motion the alchemy of healing, positive energy and empowerment.

The environmental crisis is a reflection of our spiritual crisis, a disconnection from the Love in our hearts, a disconnection from the Web of Life. I use the power of my imagination to envision a new future for the Earth, one of a change of heart. As I imagine it, it already exists and I am part of that future, a world of respect for all Life, all people and all cultures.

I become part of the change through my commitment to a path of Love and respect for all Life.

I become part of the change through what I support with my money. Our capitalist society runs on a supply and demand mentality and will evolve into an ethical and sustainable one through our support for the products that are mindful of the Earth and reflect respect for the people who make them.

I become part of the change by the thoughts I send, by the words I say and the visions I share and communicate.

I become part of the change through my prayers and meditations and by taking part in world healing and world meditation link-ups.

I become part of the change by adding my support to environmental initiatives that are already in place and also by initiating positive changes of my own and sharing these with others.

I meditate and merge with the power of the Earth beneath me. The Earth is my teacher, showing me how to give all, to trust in the natural equilibrium and beautiful symmetry of Life, to trust in the cyclic nature of flow and the natural power of creation and natural abundant goodness of Life, to trust in the regenerative force – the Earth's and ours.

I use the Internet to pursue the connections to world Peace and Earth healing link-ups so that I know when they are and can pass the dates and times on to others (see Appendix, page 275). I also look for other networks of environmental groups to keep myself informed and included in the changes I want to see happen.

We are all part of the environmental crisis and we are all part of helping our world through the crisis. Our growing awareness that we can all work together, that each one of us adds to the web of change and transformation, propels me to act, both as an individual and with like-minded people. This is my community and I consciously make the links that establish it as an integrated part of my life.

I am inspired that we can all join in and make a difference to the whole. We all hold different bits of the puzzle and we all have our own unique gifts and talents and influence to bring to the healing.

The Earth is in crisis and the future is in our hands.

I pledge to live my life with awareness and respect for the Earth, for her health and well-being and her resources; to take less and to give back.

April 25th

The Fertile Force of Daily Practice

Today I create a new Beltain shrine outside where my Peace garden is taking shape. I light lots of nightlights with the Hiroshima Peace Flame and place stones in a heart shape as I pledge my intention to listen to my heart. I plant lots of flower seeds inside the heart shape as I give Life to the vision that our respect for the Earth and the people of the Earth is an alchemical shift in the energy of the heart, in the Love we bring and the Love that increases.

The Fertile Force of Life is Unconditional Energy, which responds to whatever I bring to it. It makes no judgement about what I wish for, it simply 'is' and will go with whatever it is united with. That is my choice, my free will, and what I bring to the flow expands. So I bring Love to create more Love and I bring generosity to generate more generosity. I add positive thinking to the streams of expanding energy, seeing waves of positivity spreading outwards, visualizing generosity and Love touching the hearts of many.

When I notice that I am being judgemental or unkind in my thoughts or ungenerous in my actions, I immediately change the energy of what I am creating by consciously setting in motion a new energy, a generosity of Spirit that creates a loving circuit of new growth.

I watch this alchemy work whenever I apply it and I feel strengthened by this. I keep focused on what I give energy to, on what I fire up by my intentions and my actions. Alchemy is everywhere! I am the alchemy and alchemy is reflected in all I give Life to.

I am inspired by the Elixir of Life, our ability to be our own healing energy through the messages we communicate to ourselves and ultimately to our cells. Daily practice helps me to keep focused on this alchemy, so that I generate cycles of beneficial energy within my body. I choose a few simple but *powerful things to do every day that help me to establish new patterns. These might include repeating new positive affirmations, body work such as Yoga, etc., visualizations of health and vitality, sending daily messages or mantras to my cells, daily chakra balancing, daily meditation, daily exercise, focused contemplation, sending healing, Love, forgiveness, appreciation, gratitude and other energy catalysts to myself, to others or out into the world. By repeating the same things every day I build up layers of powerful energy and lasting transformation from the inside.*

Daily practice is a personal energizer and I keep it simple and enjoyable, only doing what I can sustain. In this way I support what I add to the flow of increase in my life. I usually do my daily practice first thing in the morning or last thing at night so that I establish a time when I automatically remember to do it.

Beltain is a good time in the cycle to establish things that will help me to stay grounded and connected to my spiritual path. So I choose to establish a simple routine of 15 minutes of automatic writing first thing every morning followed by 15 minutes of meditation, and a daily walk with a simple mantra or positive affirmation to repeat while I am walking. I also give myself a daily chakra balance last thing at night before I go to sleep. All of these things help me to stay connected to myself, to my path and to the alchemy I am establishing in my life. Their power lies in their repetition. They take very little time and the benefits are noticeable.

Daily Chakra Balancing

I begin by consciously connecting to my breath, breathing deeply and taking in my gratitude to Air. I picture the flow of Air energizing every cell in my body.

I breathe in my gratitude to Water, picturing Water flowing around my body, energizing every cell in my body.

I breathe in my gratitude to Earth for the cycle of birth, death and regeneration inherent in every cell in my body.

I breathe in my gratitude to Fire for the activation of new Life in every cell in my body.

I breathe in my gratitude to Spirit for the Unity of Life reflected in every cell in my body.

I send my inner awareness to each of my chakras in turn (see page 259), sensing how each one is feeling, what colour it might be, whether it feels light and vibrant or dull and sluggish. This is my personal check-in with myself and it provides me with clues to my essential energy and the Life Force within me.

I use my imagination to send my chakras the healing energy of Love and Light and I picture each one flowing into the next in a continuous circuit of Life, creating Unity and flow within me.

Sometimes I use the power of sound and intuitively tone the notes that harmonize and resonate with each chakra to facilitate their rebalancing.

April 30th / May 1st

Beltain Eve and Beltain Morning

We Elementals have a tradition to meet every year on the same date at the same place to celebrate Beltain and the first day of summer. We spend Beltain Eve together and walk across the fields at dawn on Beltain morning to a special copse where we can see the Sun rise.

This year the evening is clear and still and we have a bonfire at the bottom of the garden — the first bonfire of the new season! We circle the fire to energize the space. We drum, dance and sing, letting our voices express our connection to this moment, the Elements and each other. We create sacred space by singing in each of the Five Elements, echoing back to each other our notes, words, sounds and songs, letting the moment flow and weave its alchemical magic. Gradually the high energy fades and a gentle stillness descends. We hold hands and gently tone notes together, harmonizing and blending sounds, staring into the fire and looking inside ourselves for what we wish to energize here at Beltain.

I think a lot about my recent experiences of merging with the spring, the land and the Spirit of Hermes Mercurius. I stare into the fire, merge with the fire, become One with the fire and feel its bright dance within me. I send my energy up to the stars, bright in the night sky, and know that I am the stars, that their light is shinning inside me.

I know that the same spark of light that is in the stars is in this fire and in all of Life. I sing with this Light, picture it vibrating through everything – Infinite Light, Infinite Life. I am filled with a great Love for the beauty of it all and the Love fills me up. I sing out my notes, and my notes and Love join with those of my friends beside me and we fill the space around the fire with harmony and celebration.

Then we are ready to jump the fire. As we jump, we call out what we wish to energize, using the alchemy of Fire and the Fertile Force to activate what we wish to take forwards, what we wish to unite with. In the past we have called out what we wished to leave behind, but it is a more powerful alchemy to invoke what we wish to energize, to reinforce the positive through our words and images. We each jump the fire several times, energizing our future in this moment of wild, exhilarating abandonment.

After this we bless and share food and stay up late, talking and telling stories around the fire. It is such a perfect night to share with each other, watching the stars and the path of the Moon across the sky. We decide to have a few hours' sleep and to set the alarm for 4 o'clock, to stay in sacred space while we sleep and ask for guidance through our dreams.

When we wake it is cold and dark and the birdsong is faint but just beginning. We share our dreams over a cup of tea and then we are off, walking across the fields towards the woods. Now the birdsong is loud and insistent – the dawn is coming! The pulse of the Life Force is strong and everywhere Nature is manifesting the abundance of the Earth. It's wonderful to be out this early in the morning and we are full of excitement and wonder at the spring flowers, the Cowslips, Bluebells and the first Hawthorn flowers. There is a bit of cloud, but we are hopeful that this year we will see the Sun rise.

As we walk up the hill the sky is beginning to lighten and just as we reach the copse the Sun breaks free from the horizon and releases its golden light! We all break into whoops of glee and laughter and spontaneous song! A good omen!

One of our Beltain traditions is to tie ribbons in the trees as we express our Beltain visions. We have three ribbons each and we each energize a vision for the world, a vision for our community and a vision for ourselves. Our ribbons from previous years are still here hanging in the trees and after our celebration of the Sun we each slip off amongst the trees to revisit our old ribbons and to tie on the new.

For the World I tie on my ribbon as I visualize a worldwide change of heart and expanding Love in the hearts of all people.

For my community I tie on my ribbon and visualize Love and generosity of Spirit spreading amongst us.

For myself I tie on my ribbon and visualize Love and kindness guiding my decisions and actions.

After this we sing some more as we stand together under the trees in the sunshine and then walk back through the woods, which are swathed in the stunning deep blue of the Bluebells. Everywhere Life is manifesting its abundance, expressing its aliveness through each unfurling leaf, bud and flower. We too are feeling expansive as we weave through the paths in the wood, filled with our delight for the Earth and the sharing of friendship and celebration.

We arrive back and share a hearty breakfast together. We then close our circle, thanking each of the Five Elements, taking them into our hearts and sending their alchemy out into the world. We end on a Cone of Power, blending all our notes together in a great wave of sound as we send our Beltain visions on their way.

May 24th
The Garden of my Soul

I am the Web of Life and the experience of creation is in me. Every moment is an opportunity for me to participate in the natural fertility of Life through each of the Five Elements.

The natural expansion of the Life Force is also functioning at the subtle level of energy within me. At the subtle level, the energy we create is in the Ether or Spirit Realms, and this is the early stage of manifestation.

The energy I am creating adds to the whole, as all things are united in Spirit. I am aware that it is not only my actions (Fire) that are affecting the interconnected Web of Life – the energy of my feelings (Water) also has Life, as does the energy of my thoughts (Air). The shaping of the bigger picture begins here with me (Earth), with each of us. We are all responsible for the energy that is brought into the world.

What we add to the flow of energy at the subtle level becomes available for all, as all things are connected. There is a moment, known as critical mass, when the level of energy produced by a new understanding or new perception takes on a Life of its own and begins to manifest on the Earth. This is known as the Hundredth Monkey Phenomenon and is seen throughout Nature. When a critical number of creatures learn a new skill it miraculously is passed on to the whole species, despite any lack of physical contact.

I am inspired by the thought that all the people who are becoming aware of the interconnected Web of Life and are bringing Love and healing into the world are helping us to reach critical mass. Eventually, we as a race will reconnect to this essential belief in the Unity of Life.

We can all take part in this consciousness revolution by adding our Love, our positive energy and positive actions to the flow. We are creating a new awareness that we can live life in a different way, with respect and care for the Earth and all her inhabitants.

We are the people we have been waiting for and through us this future becomes manifest.

Out of this vision I create a new focus for my meditation. I visualize all the people who desire to work alchemically for change becoming joined in a web of energy around the Earth. We are aware of each other, gaining strength and trust in our individual and collective abilities to create positive change. I tune in to this image, picture all of us united and I gain strength from this. We are the people we are waiting for and together we are a powerful force for change.

This is the vision that is growing deep in the garden of my Soul. This connects me to all the other people in the world whose Love is creating transformation from the inside to the outside, from Spirit to Manifestation. We are joined through the energy of Universal Love, through the Love in our hearts. The more we connect to this Love, the more it grows in our lives and in the world.

I make the most of this fertile time to plant these seeds so that they will grow into strong healthy plants in the future. Every moment is an opportunity to set in motion what I truly want to grow and encourage. I plant and water everything that feeds my Spirit and my Soul and feeds the Spirit and the Soul of the Earth, all the things that support this vision of a change in consciousness, a change of heart. Everything we do adds to the interconnected Web of Life.

HERMES MERCURIUS

As Above, So Below
As Within, So Without

Hermes Mercurius holds this alchemical maxim up high so that I know it to be true with every part of my united being, with every breath I breathe, every thought I send, every moment I feel and every action I make. My inner world is reflected into my outer world.

This is the alchemy and Unity of Life and I am the power of this alchemy.

I am inspired to believe that true freedom lies in transcending my own self-imposed limitations of Time and dualistic thinking.

I am inspired to believe that Universal Love and Unity consciousness are powerful catalysts for change and healing.

What I believe right now in the present is the key to what happens next, as all is connected.

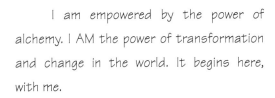

I am empowered by the power of alchemy. I AM the power of transformation and change in the world. It begins here, with me.

I am empowered by the joy that I AM the Fertile Force and whatever I give my energy to will grow and add to the whole.

I am empowered by the understanding that WE ARE the Earth, the Air, the Water, Fire and Spirit, and whatever we do to the Earth and the Life-giving Elements we do to ourselves.

I am empowered by my gratitude to the Earth, to Air, to Water, to Fire and to Spirit, to all that is giving us Life. I am empowered to create beneficial change through respect for the Earth and all Life on Earth, in any way that I can, through actions of heart and Spirit, through my thoughts, words and meditations and the energy I bring to the Web of Life. This adds to the flow of what is available for all.

I am empowered by all the people who are working for change and healing in the world. I am part of a growing network of people committed to being part of the new consciousness of inclusion, Love and respect for each other and for the Earth. Change begins with a connection to the Love in our hearts, the Universal flow of Love that joins all people together and creates Unity. We become One with the Web of Life and the healing has begun.

We empower each other! We activate a revolution of the heart that inspires us all to empower our vision for a better future by making it part of our present, by living our loving energy right now, for this IS our future.

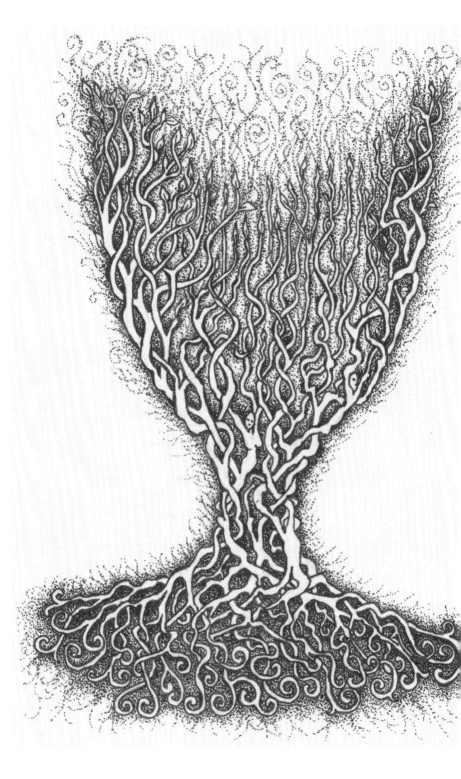

Eternal Cycles of Life

My journey through the alchemical experiences and the Celtic festivals shows me that everything I do is part of a cycle and I do nothing in isolation. Both systems help me to be part of the natural cycles of the Earth and the natural laws that govern Life. Through my journey, I am more deeply rooted in my relationship to the Earth and experience myself integrating and flowing with all Life. I am able to follow the threads of my think- ing and my feelings and staying connected to them. I keep flowing and growing in understanding and wisdom as each season takes me into a new set of possibilities. I flow in balanced cycles of inner expansion and outer expansion and apply alchemy to whatever thread I am following.

I am increasingly aware of the powerful natural forces that are at work within us and around us, the powerful yet subtle energies that are never still, constantly forming and reforming depending on what we bring to them through our thoughts, our feelings and our actions. Energy is cyclic, energy is flowing, and whatever I give to the flow returns to me. What energy I release into the flow determines what happens next. The future is in my hands, now, in this moment.

Each cycle takes me deeper, and once again as I connect to the Midsummer Solstice and the alchemical experience of Calcination, I take my understanding within to begin a new Yin cycle, building on what I have brought to Life during this one.

What we bring to each cycle continues.

Appendix

Activating the Chakras

7 Crown

6 Third eye

5 Throat

4 Heart

3 Solar plexus

2 Sacral/Womb

1 Base/Root

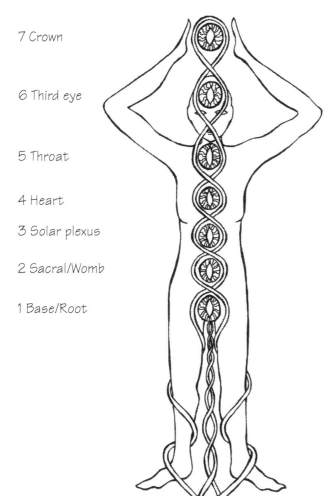

By activating my awareness of each of my chakras I am able to get in touch with the subtle energy within me. Each chakra gives me access to different aspects of myself. I unite with each of these energy points as part of developing my understanding that we are our own healers and can create our own healing from within.

There are many different techniques for energizing the chakras. A favourite of mine is to imagine the Life Force or Chi as spirals of radiating Light energizing each of the chakras in turn. I also imagine the energy flowing between the chakras so that the fullness of one brings energy to another and they form an integrated circuit of moving Chi.

Sitting comfortably, I close my eyes and begin to breathe deeply and consciously, letting the gentle rhythm of my breathing send waves of relaxation through me. I pass my breath through each of the chakra points as I let my energy drop from my busy head down through my body into the Earth. I do this for as long as it takes to feel my energy become calm and my head to empty.

Then I unite with the stabilizing force of Earth and draw this energy inside myself, creating a circuit of energy between my body and the Earth beneath me, passing the energy from the Earth up through all of my chakras to the top of my head and back down again.

I continue to breathe deeply and rhythmically. When my mind wanders I try not to follow my thoughts, just observe them and gently bring my focus back to the rhythm of my breath, feeling each chakra opening and being activated in turn.

This can then be taken further into a deeper exploration of each of the chakras. I tune in to each one, sensing where each one is in my body and how each one feels.

I ask myself, 'What are my impressions of this chakra? Does it feel full of energy or does it feel empty? Does it feel bright or is it dull and sluggish? Is it in turmoil or is it peaceful?'

From this I go on to a chakra meditation and visualization to energize and balance the chakras.

Chakra Meditation

I light a candle and dedicate it to the flow of energy between my chakras. I sit and watch the candle flame for a while until I feel peaceful and still inside and then I close my eyes and take the image of the candle flame inside myself.

I take the flame to my Root or Base chakra, which connects me to the Earth and the material world. It is also where the Kundalini serpent, the vital Life Force, lies coiled and ready, like a pilot light, to fire up and connect all the chakras together. When the Root Chakra is balanced and at One with itself, it creates stability and support for the whole body, so it is worth spending time here. Deep instinctive drives such as survival instincts, sex, fear, safety and protection are experienced here. I send my flame in wide cycles of light around this chakra, spiralling down into the Earth beneath me as my roots spread out around me and anchor me to the Earth.

Next I take the flame to my second chakra, the Naval chakra, the Womb chakra or Sacred Vessel. This is where I was once connected to my mother in her womb, an energetic cord that still connects me to the place of pure innocence and my connection to the Universal Source or Essence of all Life. This opens me to the experience of Universal Love, which I allow to wash through me, energizing me from within.

Then I open up to my Solar Plexus at the centre of my torso, the third chakra. This is the place from which I communicate and express myself, where I hold my belief patterns about myself. This is the centre of my self-esteem and my relationship to my ego. I shine the healing Light of Universal Love here, picturing spirals of energy radiating outwards and inwards at the same time, joining all the first three chakras together. I experience their united energy within me and I feel loving, open, stable and grounded. My flame becomes golden healing Light.

Gently and slowly, in my mind's eye, I move this living healing Light around my body. I picture its warm golden glow spiralling up to my Heart chakra, sending strength and stability to my emotional centre. I connect to my ability to send healing energy through Universal Love. I feel its power and uniting force and I know that I can send it to bring healing wherever it is needed.

I then take the Light to my Throat chakra, the place from which I speak my truth and live by my truth. I picture the golden Light spiralling here, releasing fluidity and flow, uniting the Universal Love in my heart to my power to express it.

From here I take the golden Light of Universal Love to my Third Eye chakra, to unite with my spiritual truth, activating my intuition and my inner sight. I picture the golden Light spiralling up and out to connect to my thoughts, bringing a Loving Awareness into my life and into the world.

I move the Light spirals up to my Crown chakra, opening my connection to Spirit and my spirituality. As I bathe my Crown chakra with golden Light I visualize all the chakras uniting and infuse them all with Universal Love and Light, creating a circuit of energy that spirals up and down my energy centres. This is the uniting energy of the Kundalini serpent, the Life Force or Chi.

I end the meditation by sending the healing flame out into the world, sending out wave upon wave of golden healing Light and Love that bring inner Peace to all they touch.

Gold

Native Gold is found in veins, deposits, crystals, cubes, octahedral shapes (having eight plane surfaces) as well as irregular or dendrite (branching, tree-like) masses. It is found as flakes, grains, plates and nuggets and has a range of colours from silvery white through golden yellow to orange red, depending on the other metals mixed with it. It can sometimes be found in other minerals such as Quartz.

Alluvial Gold weathers from the vein deposits and is washed down into rivers. It is a heavy metal and people learned how to 'pan' for Gold, swirling the water round a metal pan or woven baskets to separate the Gold deposits from the lighter sand and gravel. Pure Gold is very malleable and can be rolled and beaten into many shapes. From the earliest times it has been wrapped around other precious gems and worn as jewellery.

In all of the ancient civilizations Gold was a symbol of power and wealth. Around 3000 BC the Egyptians mastered the art of beating it thinly to make Gold leaf, casting it and using it to form alloys with other metals to achieve variations of colour and hardness. This laid the foundations for creating beautiful Gold jewellery and artefacts the world over.

Gold was valued as a great gift from the Earth Mother and goldsmiths held a special place in the community. In early times, as already mentioned, it was believed that all metals were 'growing' and would eventually become Gold. So working with Gold was seen as a sacred task and the goldsmith as worthy of working with the Spirit of Gold.

Metalworking and smithcraft were considered to be especially sacred because the ores were taken from the Earth Mother. Rituals and ceremonies accompanied mining and early miners were purified before going down into the Earth.

Smiths and metalworkers were revered as divine creators and their craft was considered to be powerful alchemy. It was believed that the Spirit of the metalworker was able to join with the Spirit of the metal and that their intention created manifestation and power in the objects he made. The early smiths and artists were seen as magicians, shaman and alchemists. They were revered as being gifted and wise and, along with the poets, musicians and dancers, were honoured for their ability to harness the elements and the gifts of the Earth to create perfection. But the smiths could use their skill with metals for creating Life-enhancing objects of beauty or for creating weapons of death.

Gold was valued not only for its purity and its unique non-corrosive property but also for its energetic presence and healing ability. It was thought to cure all diseases and prolong life, and is still used in medicine and healing today. Healers use Gold energetically to bring balance and Unity with all Life. It has been called the 'Master Healer'. Its high electrical conductivity creates an open circuit of Union between the healer and the patient, amplifying positive vibrations, happiness and healing.

Gold brings balance and harmony to the chakras, especially the Heart chakra, opening the heart to giving and receiving, opening the heart to Love. It also opens up the Third Eye chakra and the Crown chakra, amplifying connection to Spirit and restoring the harmony of mind, body and Spirit.

When used with other gemstones it enhances and amplifies their properties.

The healing properties of Gold are used by crystal healers for the treatment of blood disorders, skin problems, including skin cancer, heart disease and eye problems, to improve digestion, circulation and respiration and for the rejuvenation of the nervous system. Gold vapour lasers are used in the treatment of cancer cells and a form of medication containing Gold is used in the treatment of rheumatism or arthritis.

Gold's superior electrical conductivity, its malleability and its resistance to corrosion have made it a vital component in today's electrical products such as computers, cell phones and telephones. In computers, fine Gold wire is used to connect circuits to the semiconductors, or 'brains' of the computer. Each key strikes Gold circuits that relay the data to the microprocessor.

Gold is associated with the Sun, with radiant energy, inspiration and vitality. In alchemy the symbol for the Sun and for Gold is the same. This is a circle with a dot at its centre, reflecting the cyclic wholeness of Life, the Union of the circumference and the centre, the inner and the outer worlds, the macrocosm and the microcosm and the alchemist's maxim 'As Above, So Below'.

Gold symbolizes the attainment of dreams, the purity of spiritual truth and perfection. In our myths and legends we have the golden apples of the Tree of Life, the golden apples of Hesperides, the golden apples of wisdom found in the fabled western Isles of the Blessed. We have the elusive pot of Gold at the end of the rainbow, requiring a change of perception, a journey beyond the physical and the realization that it is not the Gold that's important, it's the journey that leads us there.

This is the same as alchemist's Gold. It is not the Gold that is important but the journey, especially the journey through the dark transformative experiences that unlock the hidden treasures of new insights and wisdom from within.

The Hiroshima Peace Flame

After Hiroshima was levelled by the atomic bomb in 1945, a young man, Tatsuo Yamamoto, collected embers left by the flames of the bomb and took them home to his grandmother. He saw it as the fire that killed his family and the rest of his people. His grandmother thought otherwise. She placed the burning flame on the family shrine and kept it alight. It became a symbol of Love for the son and husband she had lost in the bombing, and a poignant reminder of the destruction of war and desire for Peace. Slowly, Yamamoto came round to his grandmother's way of thinking.

By 1968, the Love Flame, still alight, had become famous throughout Japan. A Peace monument was inaugurated in Yamamoto's home town of Hoshino, near to Hiroshima, and other flames were kindled from it and spread out through every Japanese province. People lit their own flames from them and took them into their own homes where they prayed for Peace.

In March 2000, a Japanese musician by the name of Hiroki Okano came up with the idea of bringing the Peace Flame to the famous Glastonbury Festival in the UK. After weeks of bureaucracy, he finally got permission to bring some embers in a pocket hand-warmer. Performing with his band Tenkoo Orchestra, Hiroki displayed the Flame throughout the festival as a symbol of world Peace. On Sunday morning a candlelit and rainbow procession was led throughout the site from the Green Futures field to the main stage for a Peace ceremony.

Afterwards the Tibet Foundation invited Hiroki and his friends to bring the Peace Flame to the Tibetan Peace Garden in London to participate in a ceremony for Peace around the mandala. The Tibet Foundation in London has now taken over guardianship of the Peace Flame in England and will keep it burning and ensure that it is used to promote the message of Peace.

The Peace Flame has been travelling round the world, been included in interfaith walks for Peace and joined people of all faiths and cultures in a common wish for Global Peace. More information about this can be found on the many Internet sites relating to the Hiroshima Peace Flame.

Hiroki brought the Peace Flame to Glastonbury festival again in 2004, to the Peace Dome in the Kings Meadow.

Inner Journeying, Trance and Visualization

These are all tools for understanding, working and interacting with the Otherworld. They provide a window into the world inside my imagination, stabilizing this place for just a moment, allowing me to look inside myself and tap into forces beyond my surface reality and logical understanding.

The Otherworld is accessed through a trance-like state, an altered state or non-ordinary consciousness. This can be as simple as spontaneous daydreaming, but can also be encouraged by staring into space, emptying the mind and resting in a meditative 'state of being'. It can be reached through meditation, concentrating on the breath or staring at a single candle flame, a picture or symbol. The Otherworld is also accessed by any unchanging rhythmic patterns such as found in rhythmic poetry, chanting, drumming (especially when corresponding to the human heartbeat), dancing (again, simple repetitive steps) or any stimulus that becomes hypnotic.

We can drum for each other, chant or tone together or use a drumming CD made especially for inner journeying or shamanic journeying. These give a choice of the length of journey: 10 minutes, 15 minutes, 20 minutes or 30 minutes of steady unchanging drum beat and then a 'call back', a rapid drumbeat that energizes the journeyer to return to normal reality.

Any number of people can journey together, or a person can journey alone.

Sit or lie comfortably and have a warm blanket ready, as your body temperature drops while journeying. It is good to have a place in mind where you choose to enter the Otherworld, such as an opening in the land, a rabbit hole, a hole in a tree, a tunnel, steps leading down or alternatively an opening in the sky, a climb up a high mountain, or some kind of flight that takes you up. It is also good to have a question in mind, such as to ask for healing, or to ask for a healing symbol or for the wisdom of a Guide, Guardian, Angel or archetype. If there is nothing that strongly comes to mind, then just be open to receiving what is revealed.

The journey usually ends with the rapid drumbeat of the 'call back', where each person brings themselves back into their body and the present moment. Share the journey verbally, straightaway, in turn, without analysing the content and consider insights afterwards. In a big group, it is better for each person to write down what they remember, again without analysing it. The journey may also be anchored by painting a stone or drawing a picture. After this the journey can be analysed, peeling back the layers to see what has been understood and what has been revealed.

Always I am amazed at the perfection and synchronicity of what is revealed and what deep insights I gain from inner journeying. They seem to crystallize my thoughts, open a window, reflect my inner feelings, reveal truths and ways forward. They are a way for me to observe my unconscious mind, to make deep connections to my spiritual path. I receive clear directions and insights that give me answers to my problems. They are like waking dreams that help me to see things in a different light.

When I first began to go on inner journeys, I thought that it was 'just' my imagination and I was 'making it all up' and yet I have come to trust my subconscious imaginings and what is revealed from this experience.

Speaking from my own experiences, I always feel safe when journeying. I only journey where I feel safe and in the company of people I feel safe with. A circle of protection can be cast before beginning, visualizing the energy protection of Guardians, Allies, or Angels, as well as Light and the Five Elements. My journeys reflect my trust and openness, and I personally have never had any experiences while journeying that have been frightening or invasive. Occasionally in one of my workshops, someone might have a difficult time on a journey. Although this may bring up uncomfortable feelings at the time, it is no more harmful than a bad dream, and can be looked upon as a gift, an opportunity to explore what it is reflecting and revealing.

A spoken visualization is another type of inner journey. These can be created or read by one person to the rest of the group or read to each other if there are two of you. The scene is set and the journeyers enter into a described environment in their mind's eye. Plenty of space is left between the descriptions so that the imagination can expand into the scene. Again, these can be found on CDs and are good if you are on your own. Visualizations are often used for healing, relaxation, guided meditation and to expand awareness of the Self. For example, you may be asked to go into a clearing in the woods, to look at a tree at the centre of the clearing – and what kind of woodland, what kind of tree is at the centre, the weather and what or who else appears in the scene will provide insights into yourself and your feelings.

Another version of this is when several people lie down together with their heads together so that they can hear each other and they co-create the journey together, each adding to the description of the journey. With this kind of journeying it is good to have a goal, such as an agreed place to go, such as the Cave of the Ancients, into a forest or to a special place to meet an agreed archetype or Spirit Guide. Once at the agreed place there needs to be time and space for each person's individual question and experience and an agreed signal for making the return journey. This can be a sound, hum or note or a softly spoken 'I am ready to return.' The return journey is usually a backtracking of the journey in. Again, share the journey with each other straight away and analyse it later.

After journeying thank your guides and helpers and it is good to eat and drink something to ground your energy back firmly in your body.

The Emerald Tablet

1. In truth certainly and without doubt whatever is below is like that which is above and whatever is above is like that which is below, to accomplish the miracles of one thing.

2. Just as all things proceed from One alone by meditation on One alone, so also they are born from this one thing by adaptation.

3. Its father is the sun and its mother is the moon. The wind has born it in its body. Its nurse is the earth.

4. It is the father of every miraculous work in the whole world.

5. Its power is perfect if it is converted into earth.

6. Separate the earth from the fire and the subtle from the gross, softly and with great prudence.

7. It rises from earth to heaven and comes down again from heaven to earth and thus acquires the power of the realities above and the realities below. In this way you will acquire the glory of the whole world, and all darkness will leave you.

8. This is the power of all powers, for it conquers everything subtle and penetrates everything solid.

9. Thus the little world is created according to the prototype of the great world.

10. From this and in this way, marvellous applications are made.

11. For this reason I am called Hermes Trismegistus, for I possess the three parts of wisdom of the whole world.

12. Perfect is what I have said of the work of the sun.

Translated by J. F. Ruska

Recommended Reading

Donna Eden, *Energy Medicine: How to Use Your Body's Energies for Optimum Health and Vitality*, Piatkus Books, 2008

Masaru Emoto, *The Message from Water*, Hado Publishing, 1999

Mathew Fox and Rupert Sheldrake, *The Physics of Angels: Exploring the Realm Where Science and Spirit Meet*, HarperCollins, 1996

Cherry Gilchrist, *Everyday Alchemy: How to Use the Power of Alchemy for Daily Change and Transformation*, Rider, 2002

Patrick Harpur, *Mercurius: The Marriage of Heaven and Earth*, Squeeze Press, 1990

— *The Philosophers' Secret Fire: A History of the Imagination*, Penguin Books, 2002

Louise Hay, *You Can Heal Your Life*, Hay House, 1999

Sandra Ingerman, *Medicine for the Earth: How to Transform Personal and Environmental Toxins*, Three Rivers Press, 2000

Peter Marshall, *The Philosopher's Stone: A Quest for the Secrets of Alchemy*, Pan Books, 2001

Christine Page, *Spiritual Alchemy: How to Transform Your Life*, C. W. Daniel, 2003

Jay Ramsay, *Alchemy: The Art of Transformation*, Thorsons, 1997

Contacts

Carolyn Hillyer

The frontispiece 'Walking as Before' is taken from the album Songs of the Forgotten People by Carolyn Hillyer and Nigel Shaw. Carolyn Hillyer is an artist, musician and writer of international reputation who sings and paints of ancient spirit and hidden memory. She performs concerts with her partner and fellow composer Nigel Shaw, exhibits installations of her paintings and creates workshop journeys for women that explore our creative spirits and seek to push back our boundaries of courage and perception. More details on their website: www.seventhwavemusic.co.uk

Links

World meditation link-ups, virtual spiritual community events and astrological information.

www.crystalinks.com

World meditation and global prayer link-ups, connecting the world through live Internet webcasts for Peace.

www.souledout.org • www.worldmeditationday.com

One Million Voices for Peace

Non-profit non-sectarian organization dedicated to spreading the message and prayer 'May Peace prevail on Earth'.

www.worldpeace.org

Greenpeace

Non-violent, creative confrontation to explore global environmental problems and their causes.

www.greenpeace.org.uk

Permaculture Magazine

A quarterly magazine using the ethics and principles of permaculture and playing an active part in the developing culture of positive change.

www.permaculture.co.uk

Positive News

A quarterly newspaper of positive news from around the world.

www.positivenews.org.uk

The Transition Town Movement

Promoting people-led, community-led, social change for our changing world.

www.transitionnetwork.org

Turning the Tide

Promoting the understanding and use of active non-violence as an effective way of bringing about change.

www.turning-the-tide.org

Index

ABOUT THE AUTHOR

Glennie Kindred is the author of eleven books on Earth wisdom, native plants and trees and celebrating the Earth's cycles. She has a strong and committed following and enjoys sharing her insights through a wide range of popular workshops and talks. She is renowned for her ability to enthuse people with inspiration to engage with the natural environment and the power that we can individually and collectively create to bring about positive change, both for ourselves and for the Earth. She is co-founder of the very popular Earth Pathways Diary (www.earthpathwaysdiary. co.uk) and enjoys editing and compiling the diary each year from contributions received from artists and writers who share a Love for the Earth.

She lives in a small market town in Derbyshire with her partner Brian Boothby, where she enjoys gardening, kitchen medicine, many creative projects, her friends and family and her local community. She is active in the Transition Towns initiative. Her passions include walking the land barefoot, guerrilla gardening, travelling and being alive to the wonders and delights of the natural world. She has three adult children, May, Jack and Jerry and a granddaughter, Evie Rose.

www.glenniekindred.co.uk

Other Books by Glennie Kindred

Earth Wisdom, Glennie Kindred, 2004, revised 2011

Earth Cycles of Celebration, Glennie Kindred, 1991, revised 2013

Sacred Tree, Glennie Kindred, 1995, revised 2003

The Tree Ogham, Glennie Kindred, 1997

Herbal Healers, Wooden Books, 1999, revised 2002

Hedgerow Cookbook, Wooden Books, 1999, revised 2002

Creating Ceremony, Glennie Kindred with Lu Garner, 2002

Elements of Change, Glennie Kindred, 2009

Letting in the Wild Edges, Permanent Publications, 2013

Sacred Earth Celebrations, revised and republished, 2014

All publications are available direct from the author. All books
bought from her website are signed by the author and can be
dedicated on request. Many of the illustrations are availble as
limited edition prints, cards and postcards.

www.glenniekindred.co.uk

Printed in Great Britain
by Amazon